RAISING *Your* *Children* for CHRIST

Other Titles by Andrew Murray

RAISING
Your
Children
for CHRIST

"...and when he is old,
he will not depart from it."
—Proverbs 22:6

Andrew Murray

WHITAKER
HOUSE

All Scripture quotations are taken from the King James Version of the Holy Bible.

Publisher's note:
This new edition from Whitaker House has been updated for the modern reader. Words, expressions, and sentence structure have been revised for clarity and readability.

RAISING YOUR CHILDREN FOR CHRIST
Previously published with the title
How to Bring Your Children to Christ

ISBN-13: 978-0-88368-045-2
ISBN-10: 0-88368-045-9
Printed in the United States of America
© 1984 by Whitaker House

Whitaker House
1030 Hunt Valley Circle
New Kensington, PA 15068
www.whitakerhouse.com

---

5 6 7 8 9 10 11 12 13 14 𝖂 14 13 12 11 10 09 08 07

CONTENTS

To all parents who long to have their homes truly consecrated to God, His Word has a message of comfort and strength. It is this: God is willing to be the God of your home, and with His divine power to do more than you can ask and think. If you will open your heart in faith, God will prove Himself to be for your home all He has been to you personally.

First, you must know what He has promised to be and to do as the God of your children. Parents must surrender themselves in faith and obedience. You must expect and accept all God has promised, and do all He has commanded. This surrender of faith must definitely take place with regard to the family.

As a parent I put myself and my children into God's hands, believing that He will fulfill His promise and immediately take control. I confess that I have prevented God from working through me as He would like to for my home. I yield myself to be His loving, obedient servant. Humbly but trustingly I say, "O when wilt Thou come unto me? I will walk within my house with a perfect heart" (Psalm 101:2).

I trust that this book will help parents to meditate on God's purpose for the family. As we study the mind and plan of God, your faith will grow. Its power will be manifested both in ourselves and those for whom we are believing.

May this book be used to make our glorious God

better known, as the God of families. May this knowledge strengthen many parents' hearts to greater faith and a more complete consecration of their home life to God.

Andrew Murray

Chapter 1

THE FAMILY—AS GOD CREATED IT

"God created man in His own image, in the image of God created He him; male and female created He them. And God blessed them, and God said unto them, Be fruitful, and multiply, and replenish the earth"—Genesis 1:27,28.

God created man to reveal to the universe His own glory and perfection. Man was to resemble God in certain ways. In all he was and did on earth, man was to prove that he was indeed created in God's image and after His likeness.

The traits of that likeness were unique and wonderful. In the dominion he was to have over the earth, man was to exhibit the power of God as King and Ruler of the universe. With the great mind that man had been given for this work, the image of God as all-wise was to be seen. In man's moral powers there was to be some reflection of God's righteousness and holiness.

God Is Love

One trait of God's character remained to be set

forth: God is love. God lives not for Himself alone, but finds all His blessing in imparting His own life to others. The Son of His love was begotten of the Father from eternity. In the Son, God has filled the universe with human beings, so that the fullness of His love might flow out from them. As the Loving One, He is the fountain of life. As the Living One, He is the fountain of love. In the same way, man may have this image of God, so that his whole life may be a life of love. Man can then give life to those he loves.

In the home on earth, in the love of husband and wife, of parent and child, God wanted to reflect the love of the Father's home in heaven. The deepest secrets of the life of the Godhead in the fellowship of the Father and the Son could then be seen on earth.

It is to this last and highest trait of the image of divine perfection—man showing forth the mystery and joy of a life in love—that we want to draw special attention. Because God is Love, He needs to have some worthy object on whom His love can rest. Because He is God, the only and all-perfect One, His Son must be the only One, the Father's image, and the heir of all things. Before the world began, from eternity, God was in Him. In God's Fatherhood of Christ, His perfection is revealed to us.

The Fatherhood Of God

Man was created after that image of God which was seen in Christ. When man had fallen, Christ came to take us up into fellowship with Himself, to give us a share in His sonship and heirship, to make us, too, the children of God. In His life given to us in salvation, we, too, become the sons of God. The Fatherhood of God is the summing up of the mystery and glory of the Divine Being.

The father of the family on earth is to have the image and likeness of the divine Father. The father reflects God's image in the life he imparts to his child, and in the loving care he shows. It is in love and trust and obedience that family life on earth reflects the image of the heavenly. In the light of this divine origin and purpose of the family, we can better understand and value our relationship to our children. On the other hand, our relationship with them will strengthen our obedience and our confidence toward the Father in heaven! Every experience of the love and blessing of a home on earth is a ladder by which to rise up and get nearer to the great Father-heart in heaven. "In the beginning God created the heavens and the earth" (Genesis 1:1). The two correspond to each other—the home in heaven is the original of the home on earth.

God's Plan For The Family

The establishment of a home of love like that in heaven was to have been the highest privilege of man. However, sin came in and brought about man's ruin. The father makes the child partaker of a sinful nature, and the father himself feels too sinful to be a blessing to his child. Then, the home too often becomes the path not to heaven, but to hell. But what sin destroys, grace restores! God's grace points back to the restoration of what He intended at creation. It was God's plan for the family with its love and its training of the children to reflect the fellowship of God's home and the love of the Father in heaven.

Every parent who is aware of his own shortcomings and longs for wisdom and grace must look back to the heavenly origin of family life. The God who created it has also redeemed it and makes it new. He watches over each family with tender interest, and gives His own Father-love to every parent who desires to be the minister of His holy purpose.

If this is your desire, begin by making God's thought your thought. Begin to see the fatherhood and the family on earth as the image and the likeness of the heavenly original. Look to God as the author of your family life and count on Him to give you all that is needed to make it what it should be. Let His Father-heart and His Father-love be your security. As you trust in His adoring love, the assurance will grow that He will enable you to make your home the bright reflection of His own.

A Parent's Prayer

Lord God, You have made me a parent and given me a child of my own. I humbly confess that the perfect love and joy of heaven has not been reflected in my home. I have failed to understand my calling as a parent. Father, forgive me. I ask

You to guide and to help me in the study of Your Holy Word. Help me to realize Your purposes for me as a parent. Teach me to know You as the perfect Father. As I study Your example as the divine Parent, make me to be a true parent to my child. Let Your love and blessing rest on our home. Amen.

Chapter 2

THE FAMILY—HEAVEN OR HELL

"In the day that God created man, in the likeness of God made He him. And Adam lived an hundred and thirty years, and begat a son in his own likeness, after his image; and called his name Seth"—Genesis 5:1,3.

"Cain rose up against Abel his brother, and slew him"—Genesis 4:8.

God created man in His own likeness. The fallen Adam also produced sons in his own likeness, after his image. Unfortunately, after Adam's fall his children took on Adam's likeness. This fact shows us the fearful and universal power of sin. It was one of the wonderful traits of God's likeness that man had the power to give life to others. When sin came into man, that likeness was not destroyed, but terribly distorted. Man still had the power to bring forth children in his own likeness. When sin conquered Adam, it conquered the entire human race. It is because of this ability to reproduce that man can be renewed to become the force God uses to re-establish His Kingdom. The parental relationship has become the strength of sin. When God restores it, it will be the strength of grace.

If we want to realize the full significance of this word, "Adam begat a son in his own likeness, after his image," we must study the story of his family at the gates of Paradise. It will teach us lessons of the deepest importance in regard to the family as sin has made it.

The Parent's Sin

Let us note how the father's sin reappears and ripens in the child. "Thou shalt love the Lord thy God with all thy heart. . .and thy neighbor as thyself" (Matthew 22:37,39). In these two great commandments, we have the sum of God's will concerning us. Adam had transgressed the first, and in sinning had cast off the love of God. His firstborn refuses to subject to the second command, and becomes the hater and the murderer of his brother. With Adam's sin his nature had become corrupted, and that same nature had been imparted to his son. The child's sin was the fruit of the father's sin.

This first picture of family life that God gives us in His Word casts a dim light on our homes! Parents can often see their own shortcomings and failures in the sinful behavior of their children! When parents realize that their children have inherited their own evil natures, this should make them very patient and wise in disciplining their children. It should lead parents to seek the only cure for sin—the grace and the life that comes from above! At the same time it should urge and encourage you to believe that He will also be merciful to the fathers, and the children, too.

The Root Of All Sin

In the sin of that first child, Cain, we have the root and type of all children's sins. The family had been designed by God to be the image of the love that reigns in heaven. Sin enters the first family, and instead of it being the image of heaven, it becomes the entrance to hell. Instead of the love and happiness for which God had appointed the family, hatred and murder make it a scene of terrible violence.

The root of all sin is selfishness—separating us first from God and then from man. It even manifests itself in the little ones in the nursery. Selfishness comes in the daily activities with friends at school or play. It even rises against the parent, and refuses to give love or obedience. Love is the way to our dwelling in God and God in us. Parents should seek for this: *the reign of love in their home.* We must realize that every manifestation of a selfish or unloving spirit is a seed of the tree that bore such bitter fruit in Cain. Nothing should stand in the parent's way of removing this evil seed from their children. We must fear and root out the seeds which often ripen so terribly in later life. Our aim should be to restore our family life to what God created it to be—a mirror and a foretaste of the love of heaven.

The Parent's Responsibility

We must not forget the influence of the parent's life: "In his own image, after his likeness." These words refer not only to a blessing lost in Paradise, and to a curse that came with sin, but also to a grace that comes with redemption.

It is true that a born-again believer cannot by natural birth bring forth a child in his own spiritual likeness. However, it *is* true that what nature cannot accomplish, prayer and a life of faith can obtain through the promises and the power of God. As we proceed in our study of Holy Scripture concerning the family life, we will find one truth to be perfectly clear. That is the promise given to believing parents that their child may be begotten again after their likeness, and that God will use them as the instruments to accomplish His purposes. As faith and prayer claim the promise and the power of God, the consecrated lives of father and mother will have power to mold the lives of their children. In this way parents will prepare them as vessels of grace, and establish them in their walk with God.

Parents must be what they want their children to be. If we want to keep them from the sin of Cain, who did not love his brother, let us beware of the sin of Adam, who did not love the commandment of his God. *Let father and mother lead a life marked by love to God and man.* This is the kind of atmosphere in which loving children can be trained. Let all your dealings with the children be done in love. Angry words, sharp reproof, and impatient answers are infectious. Love demands self-sacrifice. It takes time, attention and perseverance to train our children in God's ways. When our children hear us speak of others, of friends or enemies, let the impression they receive be the love of Christ we seek to show. Father and mother should also show love and respect for one another. Their considerate and unselfish attitudes should prove to the children that love is possible and has immediate rewards.

Above all, let us remember that it is the love of God that is the secret of a loving home on earth. When parents love the Lord their God with all their heart, then family love will be strengthened. Only those parents who are willing to live consecrated lives, entirely given up to God, will receive the full promise and the blessing. If we want to make our homes a foretaste of heaven, then ordinary, half-hearted religion is not enough. Only the love of God shed abroad in our hearts and our lives will make our homes on earth in the likeness of the home above.

A Parent's Prayer

Lord God, we bow before You in deep humility. We desire to feel more deeply the terrible power of sin in ourselves and our children. Make us aware of the danger to which sin exposes our beloved home. We confess that we have failed to show that pure love which You meant to be the beauty of family life. In our relationship with You

18

and each other, and our children, forgive us for our lack of love! Do not let our children suffer because of us, as they grow up in our likeness. Deliver us from the power of selfishness, and put Your love in our hearts by the Holy Spirit. O God, bless our children with the Spirit of love. Help us to walk before them in love, that Your Spirit may use our example and our likeness to form them into Your holy likeness. May our homes on earth be to them the pathway, and the gate, to the Father's home in heaven! Amen!

Chapter 3

THE FAMILY—GOD'S INSTRUMENT

"And the Lord said unto Noah, Come thou and all thy house into the ark; for thee have I seen righteous before me in this generation"—Genesis 7:1.

"By faith Noah . . .prepared an ark for the saving of his house" (Hebrews 11:7). Noah is an example of how the faith of a believing, righteous parent obtains a blessing, not only for himself, but for his children, too. The New Testament teaching that Noah saved his house by faith is in perfect accordance with what is recorded in the Old Testament history: "Come thou, and *all thy house,* into the ark; for *thee* have I seen righteous before me." Even, Noah's son, Ham, who, as far as his personal character was concerned, deserved to perish, was saved from the flood for his father's sake and by his father's faith. This proves to us that in God's sight the family is regarded as a unity, with the father as head and representative. Parents and children are one, and it is on this principle that God will deal with the families of His people.

It was this fact, of parents and children being one, that gave sin its terrible power in the world.

When Adam sinned, all his descendants were made subject to sin and death. The flood, as well as the fall, was proof of this. We see that the children of Adam's third son, Seth, had sunk as low as the children of Cain. Seth was also a son whom Adam had begotten in his likeness, with a sinful nature to be handed down to his children, too. This gave sin universal dominion over all generations. The family was sin's greatest stronghold because children inherited the evil from their parents. The unity of parents and children was the strength of sin.

The Instrument Of God's Grace

Noah's deliverance from the flood was to be the introduction of a new age—the first great act of God's redeeming grace on behalf of a sinful world. In it God manifested the great principles of grace, which are: *mercy* in the midst of judgment; *life* through death; and *faith* as the means of deliverance.

The family was the instrument through which sin acquired its universal dominion. This principle was now to be rescued from the power of sin and to be adopted into the covenant of grace. The family would now serve as a tool to establish the Kingdom of God. The relationship of parents and children had been the means for transmitting and establishing the power of sin.

Now the family was to become the vehicle for

the extension of the Kingdom of God's grace. Many ages would have to pass before the promised Seed of the woman would be born. However, in anticipation of that holy birth the seed of God's people were used to share in the blessing of their parents. It was because of this hope that the children of righteous Noah were blessed with their father.

The man who is righteous in God's sight is not dealt with only as an individual, but in his role as a parent. When God blesses, He loves to bless so abundantly that the blessing overflows into the house of His servant. The father is more than the appointed channel through whom the child's temporal needs are met. The believing father must see himself as the appointed channel and steward of the grace of God.

We must understand this blessed truth and by faith accept God's word, "Thee have I seen righteous before me in this generation." Then, we will understand this word: "Come thou, and all thy house into the ark." God gives the assurance that the ark in which the parent is to be saved is meant for his children, too. The ark is to be the house of the family.

The blessing comes for the parent's sake, and he must be the one to bring it to pass. It is not only a promise, but a command: "Come thou and all thy house into the ark." Noah is told to see that when he enters in, they do also. God will not deal with the house separate from the parent—the parent has to bring the children into the ark.

Saved By Faith

The question may come up as to whether a parent has the power to lead his children into the ark. The answer is simple and clear: "*By faith* Noah prepared an ark for the saving of his house." God always gives grace in proportion to the duty He imposes. The believing parent must live, act, and pray with and for his children, as one who is assured that his children are meant of God to be there in the ark with him. Let us confidently trust God for the salvation of every child. Let us instruct and inspire our children with this thought in mind. Let them grow up with the awareness that to be with the father is to be with one who is in the ark. In this way the blessing cannot be missed.

Beloved parents, listen to the good news which Noah has for you: there is room for your child in the ark. The God who saves you expects you to bring your child with you. It is no longer enough to pray and hope that your child will be saved. You must accept by faith the assurance that he can be saved, and act out in obedience the command that you are to bring him in!

This can be done if you go in and live in the ark. You must bring up and train your little children there. Be separated from the world and dwell in the ark of safety. Then God's blessing will use your training of them for their salvation. Abide in Christ and let the child feel that to be near you is to be near Christ. Live in the power of the love and the life of Christ. Then your house will be to the child the ark where Christ is known and found. If you have heard that most blessed word, "Thee have I seen righteous," then let it teach you. Learn to fulfill the precept, "Come thou and all thy house into the ark."

"Thou, and all thy house"—may the word live in the heart of each believing parent!

A Parent's Prayer

O Lord, I have heard Your message telling me that since You have accepted me as righteous in Your Son, You want my children to be saved, too. I have heard Your voice of grace saying, "Come thou into the ark, and thy house." Thank You for the assurance that this promise gives to a parent's heart! Lord, open my eyes to see what Your Word can teach me. Let me see in Noah the picture of a believing parent—walking with You, believing Your Word, obedient to Your command. Let me see in the ark the type of my blessed Lord Jesus, a sure and a safe hiding place for me and my child. Lord, give me grace, like Your servant Noah, to walk with You in such a way that You may see me righteous. Help me to believe the promise of Your grace and to obey Your command. Help me to perform the work entrusted to me so that Your blessing may abide on me and my children. May it all be to the glory of Your Holy Name. Amen.

Chapter 4

THE CHILD OF THE COVENANT

"And, behold, the word of the Lord came to (Abraham), saying. . .he that shall come forth out of thine own bowels shall be thine heir. . .And he believed in the Lord; and he counted it to him for righteousness"—Genesis 15:4,6.

"Ye are the children. . .of the covenant"—Acts 3:25.

Three times God promised Abraham that He would make of him a great nation, as the sand of the seashore in multitude. When God appeared to him the fourth time, Abraham poured out his complaint before God: "Seeing I go childless. . .behold, to me Thou hast given no seed: and, lo, one born in my house is my heir" (Genesis 15:2,3). In answer the word of the Lord came to him, saying, "This shall not be thine heir; but he that cometh forth out of thine own bowels shall be thine heir." Then come the memorable words, "(Abraham) believed in the Lord; and He counted it to him for righteousness."

The Birth Of A Child

This narrative sets before us a great truth. We must realize that the longing and asking for a child as well as the reception and the birth of our children is a matter of faith. This is a special matter in which God takes the deepest interest. It is *as a parent*, and in reference to the promise of a child, that Abraham's faith is exercised and found pleasing to God. In the power of faith the natural longing for a child becomes the channel for wonderful fellowship between the parents and God. The natural seed becomes the heir of God's promise, as well as a spiritual blessing for parents.

The oneness of parents and children was revealed to us in God's dealing with Noah. Immediately after the flood Noah's son, Ham, became very wicked. Not many years passed before the whole world was practicing idolatry. The children of Noah had been born after the flesh. Before their birth God had not entered into covenant on their behalf. They had become independent men even before God made them partakers of Noah's blessing.

With Abraham God decided to deal differently. Even before his birth, the child, Isaac, who was to be included in the covenant, was the object of God's care and the parent's faith. God watches over and sanctifies the very birth of Abraham's son by His word and by faith. Everything connected with Isaac's birth deals with God's revelation and man's faith. Against nature and against hope, God

Himself gives His promise that awakens Abraham's faith and expectation of a child.

For twenty-five years this faith is tried and purified, until Abraham's soul is filled with believing expectancy. The child must truly be the child of faith and prayer—a gift of God received by faith. Before Isaac's birth, Abraham is circumcised to once again seal the covenant. This act provides clear proof that the birth of the seed of His people is holy in God's sight. God wanted to show that this is a matter of special interest to Him, the object of His promises and His blessing.

In all this God wants to teach us that before the first hope of having children, His saints are taken into covenant with Him. Parents are called to exercise Abraham's faith, and to receive their children from His hands. From birth they are to be partakers of the covenant. Even before the birth of the child, God begins the great work of redeeming love.

The Strengthening Of Faith

Before he received the promised child, Abraham had to wait a long time. God thought this waiting was necessary for the strengthening and ripening of his faith. This grace is a gift of high value and can be attained only by walking closely with God, and whole-hearted surrender to His teachings and leadings. The faith which was sufficient to justify Abraham was not sufficient to receive the blessing for his seed. Abraham's faith had to be further strengthened and purified because faith is always in proportion to the extent of the promise. Believing parents will experience that nothing so mightily quickens the growth of their faith as the reaching out after this blessing for their children. We want to have enough faith, not only for ourselves, but to impart to our children. This brings us in harmony with that law of the Kingdom: "According to your faith be it unto you" (Matthew 9:29).

Abraham's story gives us the comforting assurance that God will give the grace to attain what we need. With patience and long-suffering He led Abraham and Sarah until they were ready to accomplish His purpose. Then it could be said of them, "(Abraham) believed that he might become the father of many nations" (Romans 4:18) and, "through faith Sarah herself received strength to conceive seed, and was delivered of a child" (Hebrews 11:11).

God, who has undertaken to fill us with His Spirit, will Himself train us for our holy calling as believing parents. He will teach us how the birth of our children can become the highest exercise of a faith that gives glory to God. He will also teach us that faith is the truest means of advancing our spiritual life and the interests of His Kingdom.

The promise of God and the power of faith are the links by which our children become the heirs of the spiritual blessing. At the same time the parental relationship becomes one of the best schools for the life of faith. As believing parents we can become conformed to the image, not only of faithful Abraham, but of the Father in heaven.

A Parent's Prayer

Our blessed God and Father, we thank You for the wonderful revelation of Your will in Your servants Abraham and Sarah. Although Abraham's child was the heir of sin, You made him the heir of the promise and its blessing. Gracious God, help us to see how, through the birth of Jesus Christ, our children have been redeemed from the power of sin. Teach us to realize that You give abundant grace and faith to believing parents so that we may receive our children from You and for You. O God, enlighten our hearts to realize that the fruit of our body is to be the heir of Your promise. May we, like Abraham, let our role as parents be what binds us to You in worship and in faith. Amen.

Chapter 5

THE PROMISE OF THE COVENANT

"And I will establish my covenant between me and thee and thy seed after thee in their generations for an everlasting covenant, to be a God unto thee, and to thy seed after thee"—Genesis 17:7.

"The children of the flesh, these are not the children of God; but the children of the promise"—Romans 9:8.

There are the first terms of God's covenant with Abraham, the father of all who believe. This is the great foundation promise of what God calls "an everlasting covenant." God had already revealed Himself to Abraham as his God, and the God who would give him a child. The thing that is new and remarkable here is the assurance that the covenant now to be established was to be with Abraham's seed as much as with himself: "a God unto thee, and thy seed after thee." Let us see how this promise is the same for the child as for the parent.

The Terms Of The Covenant

The *matter* of the promise is the same in each case: "I will establish My covenant," and, "I will be a God unto thee, and to thy seed after thee." It is God's purpose to have the same relationship with the child as with the father. The believing parent and his child are to have the same place before Him. God longs to take possession of the children before sin takes over. From before the birth of the child, God wants to secure them as His own. He wants the parent's heart to be strengthened by the thought that the child is His. "A God unto thee, and to thy seed."

The *certainty* of the promise is the same. It rests on God's free mercy, on His almighty power and His covenant faithfulness. God's faithfulness to His purpose is the foundation on which the promise rests. It is the reason its fulfillment can be expected.

The *condition* of the promise is in each case the same. It is offered to the faith of the parent, and has to be accepted by faith alone. If the promise "I will be thy God," is not believed, then the promise can have no effect. God is true and His promise is faithful, but if it finds no entrance because of unbelief, the blessing is lost. This is also true of the second part of this promise: "a God to thy seed." If the parent's faith accepts this for his child, God will see to it that his faith is not disappointed.

The *recipient* of the promise is the same. It is

not as if the first half of the promise is given to the father, the second half to the child. It is the same person to whom the two parts of the promise come. In the one half, the parent accepts it for himself. In the other half, he accepts it as a father for his child, but it is one act. The promise does not have to wait for the child to believe, but it is given to the father's faith with the assurance that the child's faith will follow. With Abraham, as with each believing parent, the same faith accepts the personal and the parental blessing. The blessing is in either case equally sure, if faith continues to believe.

Believing The Covenant

It is here that a difficulty arises with many people. They see that God's promises of mercy to sinners are free and sure and find in believing them, that they come true. However, regarding their children, the promise does not appear so simple and certain. They cannot understand how one can so confidently believe for another. They know that the only sure ground for faith is God's Word. However, they have not yet been able to realize that the Word of God really means that they are definitely to believe that He is the God of their seed.

Their impressions are in accordance with views that are commonly held concerning child-rearing. They think that the salvation of their children depends upon faithful parental training. This attitude provides no absolute certainty of success. It excludes God's promises and His sovereignty. It is evident that such a general principle, with its possible exceptions, cannot give the rest of faith the parent longs for. Faith needs the assurance that God's purpose and promise are clear and unmistakeable. Only then can we trust completely in His faithfulness.

Such was the promise given to Abraham and such is the promise to every believing parent. I find my foundation of hope on behalf of my child in that very definite promise with which God, Himself, is linked. The first half, "I will be a God unto thee," is the divine pledge of the second, "a God to thy seed."

When as a struggling sinner I first sought for mercy, I did not trust in some general principle that seeking is followed by finding. Instead, I trusted in the very definite divine assurance that, "Every one that asketh receiveth; and he that seeketh findeth" (Matthew 7:8). First, I believed the promise, then I came and was accepted. I found the promise true: "I will be thy God." I am now made aware of the promise that He is willing to be the God of my seed, too. Wherever God comes with a promise, He expects faith to accept it at once.

Faith In God's Promise

The promise given to Abraham was not conditional on Isaac's believing, but it was intended to be a source of security. As I stand in covenant with my God, and see how He offers to be the God of

His people's seed, I have the right in faith to claim this promise. I can be assured of my child's salvation as firmly as my own, through faith in the God of truth.

There is another question that often troubles many, How about election? How can I be sure that my child is one of the elect? The first half of the promise again gives the solution. When I believed to the saving of my own soul, it was the things revealed in His Word, His invitation, and promise which convinced me. I was sure the election and the promise of God could never be at odds with each other. The same is true of my child. No believer in God's promise ever had to complain that God's sovereignty had hindered its fulfillment. "They which are the children of the flesh, these are not the children of God, but the children of the promise."

Only this one thing can secure grace for the child. God's free promise must be claimed and held in faith. The promise is definite, "a God unto thee and to thy seed." Let us, like Abraham, not stagger at the promise through unbelief, but be strong in faith, giving glory to God. Let us be confident that what He has spoken, He is able and faithful to perform. Let us look upon our children, let us love them and train them as children of the covenant and children of the promise—these are the children of God.

A Parent's Prayer

Lord God, thank You for the grace You have

revealed in the promise of the covenant. You take such unworthy sinners and make them Your children, and offer to provide for their children, too. You gave them the same promise once given to Your servant Abraham: "I will be a God unto thee and to thy seed after thee." Blessed be Your Holy Name! Lord, I ask You to give me grace to take this promise and trust it with my whole heart. I desire to believe that just as You have accepted me, I can be confident that You are also the God of my seed. As I yielded myself all sinful to You and You took me as Your own, I give my children, all sinful, too, to You. I believe You will take them as Your own. As I accepted Your promise for myself, I accept it for them. Give me grace now to look upon them as You do, as children of the promise. May this be what gives me courage and hope for their training on earth and their portion in heaven. They are the children of the covenant, children of the promise. Faithful is He who has promised, who also will do it. Amen.

Chapter 6

THE FAITHFUL PARENT

"I know (Abraham), that he will command his children and his household after him, and they shall keep the way of the Lord, to do justice and judgment; that the Lord may bring upon Abraham that which he hath spoken of him" — Genesis 18:19.

Faith without works is dead. Saving faith is the power of the new life that manifests itself in conduct and action. In true faith the soul becomes united to God and seeks to enter into the divine will as the surest way of becoming one with Himself. As faith grows clearer and stronger, it always sympathizes more fully with God's plans. It understands Him better, and becomes more conformed to His likeness. This is true not only of individual but also of parental faith. The higher the faith of the parent rises, the more the family will come under its power and be permeated by the spirit of godliness. Parental faith in God's promise will always be known by parental faithfulness to God's will.

Abraham is a remarkable illustration of this. As distinctly as God's Word speaks of his faith, it also tells of his faithfulness as a father. Faithfulness in his household gave Abraham access to God's secrets and to God's presence as intercessor for Sodom. When God was planning to destroy Sodom, he told Abraham about it even before it happened. Abraham was then able to intercede on behalf of his kinsmen in Sodom.

Let us try to understand what this means, and why God places such importance upon our parental faithfulness. Let us study the need, the character, the blessing, and the power of a parent's desire to do God's will in his own life.

The Need For Faithfulness

First of all, the parent *needs* to have faith. Without it the blessing is lost, and the purpose of God is made void. If God, by direct intervention or by special agents, were to seek the salvation of the little ones, then there would be no reason for the parent to take part in the covenant. God's purpose in honoring the parents in this way is to permit him to train the child for God. God seeks a people on earth, and the family is the institution for this purpose. Believing and devoted parents are one of the mightiest means of grace.

God's covenant and the parent's faith are only preliminary steps. It is the godly upbringing by the parents that leads the children into the blessings of the covenant. They must learn to know, choose, and love the God who has given Himself

37

to them. The most precious promises of God make no difference unless the child is brought up to desire and accept the friendship of the Holy One, to obey Him and keep His commandments. God establishes His covenant with parents not only to assure them of what He will do, but also to strengthen them for what they must do. They are His fellow-workers in securing the children for Him.

The Character Of Faithfulness

What God says of Abraham further gives us an insight into the true *character* of this grace: "I know (Abraham) to the end he will command his children and his household after him." The spirit of personal freedom has penetrated even into our family life. There are parents who have no place for such a word as "command," which God used here. They do not understand the heavenly harmony between authority and love, between obedience and liberty. Parents are more than friends and advisers. They have been clothed by God with a holy authority to be exercised in leading their children in the way of the Lord.

There is an age in the life of the child when his will is to a large extent in the hands of the parents. It is during those years that the quiet, loving exercise of that authority will have great influence. The idea of commanding is not in the sense of giving instructions or making demands on the child. Instead, it is the character that we see in the heavenly Father. His tenderness of affection combined with authority commands obedience. It is the silent influence of example and life which makes the child often unconsciously bow to the stronger will, and makes him happy in doing so.

The Blessing Of Faithfulness

The *blessing* of such parental faithfulness is certain and abundant. God says: "That the Lord may bring upon Abraham that which He hath spoken concerning him." If Abraham was to be blessed, and his seed with him, he must, as a faithful parent, pass on what he himself knew of God. It is only as the children become partakers of the parent's spirit that they can share his blessing. The child is to be identified with the parent in similarity of character and conduct.

This solemn responsibility may well make us tremble, but God's Word gives us divine comfort.

The Power Of Faithfulness

The *power* is provided in the purpose of God. The words of the text are most remarkable: "I know (Abraham) that he will command his children and his household." It was for this very purpose that God had chosen him and revealed Himself. God Himself was the security that His own purposes should be carried out. God knew that Abraham could do it.

Every believing parent has the guarantee that God will give the grace to prepare for the blessing, as well as the reward. We can count upon Him because he said: "I know (Abraham), *that* he will

39

command his children and his household." It is part of God's covenant that He will first teach man to keep it, and then reward that keeping (see Jeremiah 32:40). In this way the children are blessed because of a covenant-keeping God and a covenant-keeping parent. "The mercy of the Lord is from everlasting to everlasting upon them that fear him, and His righteousness unto children's children; to such as keep His covenant, and to those that remember His commandments to do them" (Psalm 103:17,18).

The Parent's Calling

There are two sides of a parent's calling. Be very full of faith and be very faithful. Be full of faith in the living God, in His covenant, in His promises for your children, and in His faithfulness. Take God's Word as the only measure of your faith. Then, be very faithful and take God's Word as the only measure of your life, especially in the family. Be a parent such as God would have you to be. Let it be your one desire to live a holy life yourself, to rule your home, to command your household and your children that they may walk in the ways of the Lord. Then the Lord can bring upon you that which He has spoken concerning you. You can be sure that the blessing will be large and full. You will be blessed in your own Christian life as well as in your home life with your children. You will also be given power, like Abraham, to enter into God's secrets, and to plead with Him as an intercessor for the unsaved.

God will prove to you that believing, faithful parenting is one of the highest privileges to which man can be admitted. Study Abraham in his fatherhood as a man chosen of God, faithful to God, and blessed of God. Find in him the type, the law, and the promise of what your role as a parent should be.

A Parent's Prayer

Lord God, You have indeed taken me, too, into this wonderful covenant. Teach me to fully realize what parental faithfulness is. I make this the one object of my home life, to train my children to serve You. By my life, by my words, by my prayers, by gentleness and love, by authority and command, I will lead them in the ways of the Lord. Please help me to do this! Teach me to understand that You have made provisions for the grace to enable me to perform my parental duties. Let my faith see You undertake for me and all I have to do. Let my ever-growing faith be the root of an ever-growing faithfulness. I ask it in the name of Your Son. Amen.

Chapter 7

THE CHILD'S SURETY

"And Judah said unto Israel his father, Send the lad with me. . .I will be surety for him; of my hand shalt thou require him"—Genesis 43:8,9.

These are the words of Jacob's son, Judah, when he tried to persuade his father to send Benjamin to Egypt with him. Judah's becoming surety for the child meant that he was guaranteeing Benjamin's safety and return. Judah was ready at any sacrifice to fulfill his duties. This is evident later from his pleadings before Joseph. At that time Judah said, "Thy servant became surety for the child unto my father" (Genesis 44:32). And he offered himself as a slave in his brother's place. In this way, Judah was a type of his own descendant, the great Surety of His people, Jesus Christ, who gave Himself for us. Judah also symbolizes the spirit of self-sacrifice of every parent to whom God commits the care of a child on his dangerous journey through life. The language and conduct of Judah will teach us some important lessons about caring for the little ones who have been entrusted to us.

who have been entrusted to us.

The Duties Of A Surety

Consider the *duties* of being a surety or guarantee for someone else, as illustrated in Judah. He was very serious about the responsibility he had undertaken. When the governor of Egypt had commanded that Benjamin should be kept as a slave, Judah at once came forward as a substitute. Not for a moment did he think of his own home and children, or of Egyptian slavery and its hardships. Everything gave way to the thought, My father entrusted him to me, and I am surety for the lad. With the most touching earnestness he pleads to be taken instead of the boy: "Thy servant became surety for the lad unto my father. . .Now therefore, let thy servant abide instead of the lad as a bondman to my lord; and let the lad go up with his brethren. For how shall I go up to my father, and the lad be not with me?" (Genesis 44:32-34).

If Christian parents would only realize as Judah did, that they are surety for their child! What do we do when our children are in danger from the prince of this world? What do we do when the temptations of the flesh threaten to make them slaves and hold them back from ever reaching the Father's home? How often are we careless or unwilling to sacrifice our ease and comfort in seeking to rescue them from their danger? How often are the spiritual interests of the child considered of little importance compared to worldly prospects of position or profit? How often do we forget the solemn covenant in which we agreed to make sure that the child is not lost to the Father in heaven?

We are so slow to realize the importance of a life of pure and whole-hearted devotion, in which selfishness and worldliness are crucified. It is only as our life is lived for God that we can really train our children for heaven! When danger threatens, and our children appear to be growing up unconverted, we must learn to bow at the foot of God's throne. We must bow until we see that our plea, "I am surety for the child," has touched the heart of the King, and we have His word to set him free. The ruling principle of parental life and love must be, "Without the child I will not see my Father's face."

The Parent's Reward

Consider the *encouragement* that the example of Judah gives us. It sets before us the abundant reward that the faithful parent will reap. In pleading with the ruler of Egypt, Judah thought he was dealing with a stranger, a cruel dictator, and an enemy. Little did he know that his pleadings were entering the ears of one who was his own brother. He never dared to hope that his plea would have such powerful influence. He did not know that the ruler would fall weeping on Benjamin's neck, saying, "I am Joseph." What a wonderful picture of the power and the reward of one who is willing to sacrifice himself and plead for another's salvation.

The parent who is praying for his child can

expect even greater rewards. If we could realize the sinfulness of our children's nature, and the dangers surrounding them, we would fervently plead with the great King and Savior for their salvation. It is then that the blessing would come to us. At first we may have no idea of the tender relationship that Jesus has with us and our children as a brother. Our reward comes in the blessed revelation of who Jesus is to us and the child.

In the experiences of many parents, we have proof that, while they only thought of obtaining what their children needed, their prayer led to experiences of the power and love of the Savior. They were brought into closer and more intimate fellowship with Him. They experienced greater personal blessing than they had in only praying for themselves. They saw Him, with whom they had been pleading, descend from His throne and say, "I am Jesus." They saw Him embrace their beloved child and kiss him. Jesus was gloriously revealed to them when as parents they appealed to Him for their children.

Jesus, Our Surety

Judah then came to understand that Joseph was the true surety for the sons of Israel. In the path of suffering, Joseph had won the throne and become their deliverance from famine and death. Parents will also learn that the more they seek to fulfill their duties as sureties, they will come to know and rejoice in Jesus as *their* Surety. He has not only undertaken their own personal salvation, but He has secured the grace they need to fulfill their duties. Jesus is the Surety for their suretyship, too, because theirs is grounded in His.

The principle on which redemption rests is that Jesus died, "Once for all." The image of humanity as a whole is found throughout the Scriptures. It especially appears in the teachings concerning the family. There the father is head, priest, and king over his own house, even as Christ is King. The father is, in a limited sense, surety for the child. When the father as the surety on earth draws near to the King, he discovers in Him the Great Surety. This revelation will give him new confidence and strength and joy in the work he has undertaken. In the light of the redemption and love and friendship of Jesus, the thought, "I am surety for the child," will gain new brightness.

It is then that the parents' devotion to the training of the children will become more earnest. They will be ready to make any sacrifice to save their children from the world. Their pleadings of faith will become more confident and triumphant. They will find richest blessings for themselves and their family in the words, "I am surety for the child."

A Parent's Prayer

Blessed Father, we ask you to open the eyes of the parents of Your Church to realize our blessed calling. May we understand that You say to us at the birth of each little one entrusted to our care,

"At your hands will I require it." May we understand and give the answer, "Of my hand Thou shalt require him. I am surety for the child."

Oh Lord, show us the dangers that surround our children. Give us the true surety spirit, the willingness to sacrifice all, rather than be unfaithful to our children. As we see the power of sin and of the world threatening them, may we plead as for our own life, that the children may be saved from sin and Satan. May our one desire be that they may be completely Yours. Let this be our one aim in prayer, education, and conversation. Lord Jesus, teach us that as You are our Surety, we are the surety of our family. You who are the faithful Surety make us faithful, too. Amen.

Chapter 8

THE PARENT'S FAITH

"And when she saw him that he was a goodly child, she hid him three months"—Exodus 2:2.

"By faith Moses, when he was born, was hid three months by his parents, because they saw he was a proper child; and they were not afraid of the king's commandment"—Hebrews 11:23.

The story of Moses will lead us a step further in the study of the way in which the faith of parents manifests itself in dealing with their children. It was faith that saw the goodness of the child Moses. It was faith that did not fear the king's wrath. It was faith that hid the child and saved his life. In each child born to believing parents, faith sees the same goodness, meets the same danger, and finds the same path of safety.

A Goodly Child

It was by faith Moses' parents *saw he was a goodly child*. The natural love of a parent's heart made the child a beautiful one in his mother's eyes, but faith saw more than nature could. God opened their eyes, and they recognized something special, a spiritual beauty that made their child especially precious. The eye of faith sees in each little one a divine goodness.

Each child is a being created in God's image, with the faint light of a divine glory shining from it. Is not every infant the object of the joy of angels and God's everlasting love and pleasure? Does not each child's worth exceed that of the whole world? Even in this life a child can be a brother of Jesus, a servant of God, a blessing for mankind. Faith sees the little one as a jewel shining in the crown of the Lamb. We have a surer hope than Moses' parents ever had and a brighter light in which the heavenly beauty of our little ones is reflected. Father, open the eyes of all Your people so that their faith may see each little baby as a goodly child.

Faith Does Not Fear

It is faith that sees, but *fears not the danger*. Our children are still exposed to the same danger. Pharaoh had commanded that the children of God's people be destroyed. He knew that if the children were cut off, the people would soon die out. Then there would be no danger of war with them and, by a slow-but-sure process, the nation of Israel would be cut off.

The evil prince of this world still uses the same tactics. When parents take a decided stand for God, the world may despise or hate them, but it soon learns that it is of little use to attempt to conquer them. However, Satan knows a surer way. The spirit of the world claims possession of the children. All too often Christian parents expose their children to the dangers of the world. Children are allowed to grow up in comparative ignorance about the blessed Savior. They are entrusted to the care of ungodly or worldly teachers. They are allowed to associate with those whose spirit and influence is altogether worldly.

The Church is often too faithless or weak to warn against this danger. The Church has failed to realize the importance of the role of parenting in the spiritual life of the child. Unfortunately, the education of the young has been left to the government, to the secular school, and to the spirit of the age. The result is that the youthful heart has lost the simplicity and tenderness of which the Master spoke when He said, "Of such is the kingdom of heaven" (Matthew 19:14).

Thousands of children of the Kingdom are drowned in the mighty Nile of this world—lost in the fruitful stream of its pleasures and profits! If only the eyes of God's people were opened to the danger which threatens His Church! It is not infidelity or superstition, *it is the spirit of worldliness in the homes of our Christian people*! The children are sacrificed to worldly ambitions and social pressures. The greatest dangers to Christ's Church are friendship with the world and the seeking of riches. If every Christian home were a training school for His service, more spiritual growth would take place than could be accomplished through preaching.

Faith Finds Safety

It is faith that still finds *the same path of safety*. "By faith Moses was hid by his parents." They trusted God on behalf of this goodly child, who was one of the children of His covenant. "By faith Moses was *hid* by his parents"—these simple words tell us our duty, and what our faith must do. Christian parents, hide your child! Hide him in that safest refuge—"the shadow of the Almighty" (Psalm 91:1). Every day lay your child in God's keeping and let your soul be filled with the knowledge that He has indeed taken charge of it. Let the love of Jesus be the first place of safety to which you guide his youthful feet.

Hide your child in the quietness of home life away from the excitements of the world. In that *hiding* place where the enemy cannot intrude, we have one of faith's highest duties. When the time comes that your child must come into contact with the world, you can still entrust him to the One who is the Keeper of Israel. Do not fear the sayings of others who proclaim, that the children cannot be kept separate from the world, they must go with the stream. Instead, let your faith be strong. Believe that yours are the children of a peculiar people, who are separated unto God. Continue to believe that they must be kept separate for Him.

The Reward Of Faith

The *reward* of the faith of Moses' parents will be ours. Moses was not only saved, but he became the savior of his people. Your child, too, will not only be blessed, but he will also be made a blessing. However, each child does not have the calling of a Moses. In His Kingdom God needs not only a Moses, but a Moses' mother and a Moses' sister for the fulfillment of His purposes. If you let your faith do its work, as Moses' mother did, then God, Himself, will see to it that your labor is not in vain. The education that Moses' mother gave her son during the years of his childhood was so successful that all the years of his training at Pharaoh's palace could not erase it. His mother's faith bore fruit in his faith, when later he, at every cost, chose suffering with the people of God. Moses was not afraid of the wrath of the king, because he saw Him who is invisible.

Let faith hide the child in the ark of God's love. Let faith, train the child for God and His people. Then, when the time comes that your child must go into the world, he will be safe in the power of faith and of God's protection. A child of faith will not only receive a blessing for itself, but be a blessing to others.

God grant that the Church may indeed become a "Moses' mother," the faithful nurse of the children He entrusts to her care, "hiding" them and keeping them separate from the world and its influence. God will give a wonderful fulfillment of the promise, whenever He finds the fulfillment of the duty: "Take this child, nurse it for me: I will give thee thy wages" (Exodus 2:9).

A Parent's Prayer

I acknowledge, Lord, that I do not fully realize the value of my children, nor the danger to which they are exposed from the Prince and the Spirit of the world. Lord, teach me to fully recognize the danger and yet never to fear the commandment of the King. Open my eyes to see in the light of heaven that each little one is a goodly child, entrusted to my keeping and training for Your work and Kingdom. Help me to keep them sheltered, to hide them from the power of the world and of sin. May my own life be the life of faith, hid with Christ in God, that my child may know no other dwelling place. Grant this also to all Your people, O my God. Let Your Church awake to know her place in this world, and her calling to go out to the land to which God has called her. Let the mighty power of faith be seen in the training of our children to show the difference between those who fear You and those who do not. Give us grace to raise our children for You. Amen.

Chapter 9

HOUSEHOLD SALVATION

"Take every man a lamb, according to the house of their fathers, a lamb for an house. . .When He seeth the blood. . .the Lord will pass over the door, and will not suffer the destroyer to come in unto your houses"—Exodus 12:3,23.

It has often been pointed out that, of all the Old Testament sacrifices, there is none that gives a clearer or richer revelation of the person and work of our Lord than the Passover. It has often escaped observation how the whole institution of the Paschal Lamb was aimed at deliverance, not of the individuals, but of families. This deliverance dealt not with the persons, but with the families, the houses of God's people. What else is the meaning of the expression, "A lamb for an *house*?" The people were told to, "Take you a lamb according to your families" (Exodus 12:21). Furthermore, the blood of the lamb was to be put upon each house. (See Exodus 12:7,22.)

This same idea is also expressed in God's

instructions to the people of Israel. "When your children shall say unto you, What mean ye by this service? That ye shall say, It is the sacrifice of the Lord's Passover, who passed over the *houses* of the children of Israel, when He smote the Egyptians and delivered our *houses*" (Exodus 12:26,27). Among the Egyptians it was the *firstborn* in every house who died, as representing the house. In Israel it was also the *firstborn* who through the blood was saved from the impending danger and consecrated for God.

God lays down this fundamental law in the Passover and the bloodsprinkling: I deal with you, not as individuals, but as families. As I chose and blessed you, as the seed of your father Abraham, so I still bless every household through the believing father, who sprinkles blood in obedience to My command. The lamb and its blood are the consecration of the homes and the family relationships of My people. In the hands of the father, God thus places the destiny and the safety of the whole house.

Christ, our Passover, is slain for us. We love to trace how the foreshadowings of the Paschal Feast were fulfilled in Him. Christ, the Lamb of God, is still "a lamb for an house." His blood may still be sprinkled upon the door so that the destroyer cannot enter in. In the new covenant, and with the precious blood of Christ, the principle still holds good: it is the believing father's right and duty in faith to appropriate the blood for his whole house. The father's faith has the divine guarantee, and will be rewarded with the divine blessing.

Cleansing Power Of The Blood

As we think of the precious blood and seek to walk in the nearness to God which it gives, let us claim its cleansing power for our houses, as well as for ourselves. Let us be assured that our faith as parents has power and does secure divine blessing. Every day there is sin in my house. The fullness of the application of the blood will correspond to what faith claims. I have in nature transmitted sin and death—through me they inherit it. Thank God, as a father, I may also transmit the grace and blessing of redemption.

Not only my own soul, but my house can daily be kept under the sprinkling and cleansing of the blood. Each time I enter my door, or think of Satan entering it, I can see it sprinkled with the blood of the Lamb. Parents and children together stand under the cover and protection of the blood: the Lord is our keeper.

Consecrate Your Family To The Lord

Every year in Israel parents had to renew the sprinkling: the blood of the Lamb has been shed once for all. I can now, each day, renew the consecration of my house to the Lord saying in the assurance of faith, ''The blood saves me and my children.'' In this faith I may confidently expect that the redemption of the blood will exercise its mighty influence to sanctify our home life and our family relationships. I can also expect our house to be wholly the Lord's, and each child to be one of His redeemed.

To accomplish this I must notice carefully how God commanded the parents to teach these things to their children (Exodus 12:26,27; 13:14). The salvation which is secured for the child in redemption must be appropriated by him personally before it is made his own. This cannot happen without the child knowing it. The children of Israel were to be taught that they belonged to the redeemed people and that they belonged to the redeeming God. The parent was to act not only as priest, but also as prophet and teacher. As he dealt for the child with God in the blood-sprinkling, so he was to deal for God in the instructions given to the child. Let us teach our children what the blood has done for them, to make them know and love the God who accepted them, even before they knew Him.

Teach Your Children God's Command

Every year the believing Israelite had to sprinkle the doorposts with blood. In this way he testified that it was only in the blood that he and his house could stand before God. He also had to write upon these same blood-sprinkled doorposts the words of God's law (Deuteronomy 6:7-9). In all the comings and goings of His children, they would see these words and be reminded that the freedom from Egypt's bondage was a freedom to serve God. God wants to be not only trusted but obeyed. We have been chosen "unto obedience and the sprinkling of the blood of Christ'' (1 Peter 1:2).

I must train and educate my children to know, and love, and keep the commands of their God. Day by day, in teaching and living, I must seek to set before them the joy of a faith that freely accepts all that God gives, with a surrender that gives all He claims.

"A lamb for an house." I must pray that God's Holy Spirit will reveal all the truths that cluster round this blessed word. It speaks of a father redeemed by the blood and his children through him partaking of the sprinkling. It speaks of the father as God's minister who must every year sprinkle the house. The father is also God's witness and messenger to the children to teach them of this precious blood and of the God it reveals. Such is God's wonderful provision for getting full possession of His people and making the family the foundation of the Kingdom.

A Parent's Prayer

Blessed Lord Jesus, the Lamb of God, Your blood cleanses from all sin. In humble faith I claim that blood for myself and my children. May my own experience of its cleansing power every day grow fuller and clearer. May I by Your Holy Spirit realize fully my right to claim it for my house. Gracious God, who gave this wonderful ordinance of a lamb for a house, I yield myself to You as the minister of Your covenant. Use me, my God, to save my children, to train them for You and You alone. I want my children to grow up to serve You.

May our faith in the blood and surrender to Your will be as the two doorposts between which we daily go in and out. The Lord make it so. Amen.

Chapter 10

THE PRIEST IN THE HOME

"And it shall come to pass, when your children shall say unto you, What mean ye by this service? That ye shall say, It is the sacrifice of the Lord's passover, who passed over the houses of the children of Israel in Egypt, when He smote the Egyptians, and delivered our houses"—Exodus 12:26,27.

The Passover sets the believing parent before us in two aspects. First, it *deals with God* on behalf of the children and brings down the blessing on them. Second, it *deals with the children* for God and seeks to lead them up to Him. In the first capacity, the parent sprinkled the blood of the lamb upon his house, securing God's protection for the children. In the second, the parent had to instruct his children, telling them of what God had done, and seeking to lead them to the personal knowledge and acceptance of this God as their God. These two parts of parental duty are closely and inseparably linked to each other, the first being necessary as the root and origin of the second.

The parent's work as priest equips him for his work as prophet and teacher. It was after having sprinkled the blood for himself and his child that the parent had to teach the meaning of this holy mystery. The parent's relationship with God, his experience of God's blessing on himself and his child, were his own training to equip him for the training of his child. As we keep this in mind, we will recognize the beauty of the family in which God has chosen and appointed the believing parent as the instructor of his children. We will realize how the parent's role provides the best way of securing a godly seed for the Lord.

The Parent As Priest In The Home

It is the parent, *who has himself already experienced the salvation of God*, who is appointed to lead the child to know God. The knowledge of God is not simply a matter of the understanding. It is to love Him, to live in Him, to experience the power of His presence and His blessing. The man who would teach others to know God must be able to speak from personal experience of Him. He must prove by the warmth of love and devotion that he loves this God, and receives his life from Him.

When God instituted the family as the great instrument for transmitting deliverance, He revealed Himself to each head of a family as the God of his salvation. In the other sacrifices in Israel, it was the priest who sprinkled the blood in

61

the holy places; but in the Passover, it was *each father* who sprinkled it *on his own house*. He, thereby, performed the act of faith by which the destroyer was kept from his house. When he went forth from Egypt and undertook the journey to Canaan, the father witnessed God's faithfulness and effectiveness regarding the atoning blood of the lamb. The father could speak as a living witness from personal experience. As a redeemed one he could tell of redemption and of the Redeemer-God.

Only personal experience of the power of the blood can qualify a parent to speak to his children of God. It is the parent who has himself experienced redemption who can tell his child about the God of redemption. This parent can then act in accordance with God's word: "And thou shalt show thy son in that day, saying, This is done because of that which the Lord did *unto me* when I came forth out of Egypt" (Exodus 13:8). Every year the parents in Israel had to renew the remembrance of their deliverance. Now, the parent who lives in the experience of Christ's redemption can speak of the mercy of the God of salvation.

The Parent As Minister

The believing parent has also been accepted as God's appointed minister in the redemption of the child. In sprinkling the blood upon the door of his house, he also saved his child from the destroying angel. He was honored to act with God on behalf of the child. What the child could not do, the parent did for him, and the deed was accepted by God. The child had initially been made partaker of the blessing of that sprinkling of blood. Later, when he grows up, the child must personally accept what has been secured and sealed for him.

The believing parent can look upon his child in the light of that great transaction between God and himself, of which that child has been the object. The parent no longer speaks to him as a stranger to the covenant of grace, but as a child of the covenant. The parent points him to a God who began to deal with him in infancy. He shares the reality of the covenant made between God and himself through the blood of Jesus Christ. The parent tells his child how God dealt with the families of Israel to bring them all to deliverance and salvation. By telling the child how he has believed and prayed for him, the parent lets him know that he cannot permit a member of his family to refuse to acknowledge the God of his house.

This does not mean that the parent should stop pleading with God on behalf of the child. The parent continues to remind the great Jehovah of the blood and the oath of the covenant, and claims for his child the blessings of redemption. Because he knows that his child has been received with him into covenant, the believing parent qualifies as the minister of God's grace to his child.

The Parent's Natural Relationship

There is another way in which God uses the family to accomplish His purposes. That is in the natural relationship between parent and child. In nature they are one, united by the closest and most precious ties. The child has his life from the father. The father looks upon the child as part of himself, of his flesh and of his bones. He loves and cherishes his child. This love seeks, even in nature, the happiness of the child, and can often make great sacrifices to attain it. It is this love which God uses in the parental covenant. It is this love which purifies the parent to be the minister of God's grace.

With a parent's love there is a parent's influence. The weakness of the child makes him dependent, to a large degree, upon the parent's will. The character of childhood is formed and molded by impressions. Constant companionship with the parent can make these impressions deep and permanent. The child's love for the parent rises and meets the parent's love. The spirit of the parent can in large measure be breathed into the child.

Of all the instruments which God uses, there is none more wonderful or more beautifully adapted to its objective than this relationship between a godly parent and his child. A parent who is made partaker of God's love and grace himself, accepted and blessed with the promises of the covenant and the Spirit, comes into covenant for his child. Then, in the power of parental affection, God uses all the influences of family life to do the great work of gaining the child for God. This surely is one of the most wonderful examples of God's grace upon earth.

A Parent's Prayer

Lord God, open the eyes of the parents of Your Church to their calling, that they may honor You as the God of their families. Lord, bless my own home, and give me grace as one of Your redeemed ones, to train my children for their God. May the joy of a personal experience of redemption and the love of the blessed Redeemer, warm my heart, inspire my words, and light up my life to testify of You and train them for You alone. Amen.

Chapter 11

GIVE GOD YOUR BEST

"And the Lord spake unto Moses, saying, Sanctify unto Me all the firstborn. . .all the firstborn of man among thy children shalt thou redeem. And it shall be when thy son asketh thee in time to come, saying, What is this? that thou shalt say unto him, By strength of hand, the Lord brought us out from Egypt,. . .And it came to pass, when Pharaoh would hardly let us go, that the Lord slew all the firstborn of Egypt. . .therefore I sacrifice to the Lord all that openeth the matrix (the womb), being males; but all the firstborn of my children I redeem"—Exodus 13:1-2, 13-15.

"Let My people go that they may serve Me" (Exodus 8:1)—in these words so often repeated by the Lord in sending Moses to Pharaoh, we see how service is the aim of redemption. God sets His people free from the bondage of Egypt to translate them into the liberty of His service—the willing, loving, free service of a redeemed people. The deeper God's people enter into the spirit of redemption, the deeper will be their insight into the blessed unity of liberty and service. There is no true service of God without liberty and there is no true liberty without service.

We have seen in the Passover what a permanent place the family and the children have in redemption. Like their parents, they were redeemed to serve. All their training was to be a training to the service of God. Pharaoh said to Moses after the plague, "Go, serve the Lord your God; but who are they that shall go?" The answer was very distinct, "We will go *with our young* and with our old, with our sons and with our daughters" (Exodus 10:8,9). It was on this point that the negotiations were broken off. The going of the children was what the king would not consent to: "Let the Lord be so with you, as I will let you go, and your little ones: look to it, for evil is before you" (verse 10). Later, when Pharaoh still wanted to keep their property, he felt that this at least must be conceded: "Go ye, serve the Lord; only let your flocks and herds be stayed; *let your little ones also go with you*" (verse 24). The future of the nation must be secured for God. A people who really want to serve God must, in the first place, take care of the little ones.

The Importance Of The Firstborn

After the people had left Egypt, the very first command God gave to Moses was in regard to the firstborn, who were to be separated and sanctified for Him. In each family the firstborn son was considered the most important and the best child. The father looked upon him as Jacob said of Reuben: "Thou art my firstborn, my might, and the beginning of my strength" (Genesis 49:3).

To the firstborn belonged the birthright and the place of honor in the family. He was the representative and head of all the children. God looked upon Israel as His firstborn among the nations. Because Egypt oppressed Israel and would not let the people go, God slew Egypt's firstborn. Now in commemoration of this act, and as a pledge of God's claim on all the children and the whole people, every firstborn belonged to God, and was set apart as His peculiar property.

For what reason was this done? For none other than for His service. This is seen with great distinctness when the tribe of Levi was taken for service instead of all the firstborn of Israel. "The Levites (shall) go in to do the service of the tabernacle. . .for they are wholly given unto Me from among the children of Israel. . .instead of the firstborn of all the children of Israel, have I taken them to Me. For all the firstborn of the children of Israel are Mine" (Numbers 8:15-17). The redemption offering of money had to be paid at the birth of each firstborn for his release. By this act the parents had the unceasing reminder that the firstborn belonged to God and His service and were represented in the Levites.

The principle involved in this is one of deepest importance. *God claims our best children for His own direct and immediate service.* All the people, both old and young, were to serve Him. However, the firstborn, the very best, were to be entirely set apart for the special maintenance of that service. They were set apart not only for the ministry of worship, but also to instruct the people in the law of their God. Let us try to take in fully the lessons the Christian Church has to learn from this.

The Need For Christian Workers

In Israel all the firstborn and all the children of Levi, a twelfth part of the whole nation, were exclusively claimed by God to be continually at His disposal in the service of His house. In Israel that service consisted solely in the maintenance of what already existed. Nothing had to be done for the extension of the Kingdom or the propogation of the knowledge of God among the heathen.

The Christian Church has to see to it that she maintains her hold on what she had already occupied in her redemption from sin. At the same time the Church must teach all the nations and seek the extension of the Kingdom throughout the whole world. The question is naturally suggested: If Israel had to set apart one-twelfth of its children for the work of God, what portion of her people should the Christian Church devote to the work committed to her? What portion *has* she devoted?

The answer to the latter question is sad! There is hardly a missionary or evangelistic organization engaged in teaching and rescuing the lost that does not complain of lack of laborers. The call is being sounded louder every year that the doors to the hundreds of millions of heathen are opened wide, and yet how sadly few is the number of laborers. Why is this? Simply because Christian parents do not, as a rule, educate their children under the conviction that they are the Lord's. They do not place them at His disposal, do not train them to look upon this as their highest privilege—to be found worthy to take the name of Christ to the unsaved.

Let us just think for a moment what would be thought of the loyalty of Englishmen to their Queen if it were difficult to find men to be her bodyguards, or accept appointments in her service! What would we think of the enthusiasm of an army where the general could never obtain volunteers for a post of danger and of honor? Jesus Christ, our King, has said that those who forsake all for His and the gospel's sake are His guards of honor. While in every profession there are complaints of more applicants than openings, the Master has to wait for workers to apply. His work has to suffer because His people do not understand that they and their children have been redeemed to serve Him who gave Himself for them.

Devote Your Children To God's Service

What is the solution to this problem? What can we do, each in our own way, to wipe out this terrible reproach? Let us devote every child to God and His service. Let us stop praying that our children will be saved if we are not willing to offer them for His service. Let us cease choosing honorable and lucrative professions for our children, with the idea that they can serve God in any calling. Let us lay each child upon the altar, especially our firstborn and our best. Let us seek this one thing—that they may become worthy and equipped to be set apart for the service of the King.

Let the Church learn as part of her preaching of redemption to lift aloud her voice and cry, "You are redeemed for service, you and your children!" Is not this the reason that so many parents have prayed for the salvation of their children and been disappointed? Their prayer was utterly selfish because it was simply their desire to see the child happy, without any thought of the glory of God, or of consecration to His service.

When God established His covenant with Abraham and gave him Isaac, it was to have him at His disposal as the channel of blessing to the world. When God rewarded the faith of Moses' parents, it was because He wanted a servant by whom He could save Israel. When God redeemed Israel's firstborn in the night of the Passover, it was to have them for Himself.

Christian parent, when God offers to be to your children what He was to Isaac, and Moses, and Israel's firstborn, it is because *He wants them for His service,* His blessed service of love and liberty. He gave His Firstborn, His Only begotten, for you and your children. Can anything be too precious for Him? Do not listen to the thought that the demand is too hard or the sacrifice too great.

71

Know that for yourself, as for your children, it is the path of honor and blessing. Let your example teach the Church that there are those who, because they love their children most intensely, know nothing better for them than to yield them to the will and the work of their God.

A Parent's Prayer

Lord, You want to have our children for Your service. We acknowledge Your claim. Let them all be used for Your service and glory, we especially offer You the first and the best. Lord God, teach us to feel deeply that You need them for the building up of Your Kingdom. We give our children to You. We will train them for You. Fill them and us with love for Jesus and love for lost souls, that they may serve You as Your Son did and give their lives to save others. Lord God, who has redeemed us and our children by the blood of the lamb, let our firstborn, let all our children, be holy unto the Lord. Amen.

Chapter 12

CHILDREN AND THE SABBATH

"The seventh day is the sabbath unto the Lord thy God; in it thou shalt not do any work, thou, nor thy son, nor thy daughter"—Exodus 20:10.

One of the most precious blessings a child going out into the world from a godly home can take with him is the habit of reverent observance of the Sabbath. If he is a Christian, it will be one of his surest aids in the growth and strengthening of his life of faith. This is part of a parent's duty that needs to be studied in earnest prayer. The performance of this duty requires wisdom and grace.

Note in the words of the fourth commandment how the children are especially remembered. It is to parents this command is given. If their children, as well as themselves, keep the day holy, then their obedience is manifested: *"Thou, nor thy son, nor thy daughter."* It is not so much as a personal, nor as a national, but as a family ordinance, that the Sabbath was first of all appointed. "Thou, nor thy son, nor thy daughter:" just as in the terms of the covenant, "a God to thee and to thy seed.''

These words suggest the two thoughts that it is first the parent, then the child, through the parent, with whom God wishes to deal. The parent must first learn to keep the Sabbath day holy himself, then to train his child to keep it holy, too. This is the principle which lies at the root of all true education: What I am to make my child to be I must first be myself. Being an example is more than rules and teaching. What I am and do is more than what I tell him to be or do.

The question is often asked how we can teach our children to respect and love the Sabbath. In answer to this question, many lessons of great value can be learned.

Parents Must Keep The Sabbath

The first requirement is that the Sabbath should be a holy day for the parents themselves. That day should be to them a day of joyful worship, of quiet devotions, and of loving fellowship with God. As the Sabbath becomes a delight for them, then the first condition will be fulfilled for teaching their children to love it.

Let Christian parents take note of this. God wants the Sabbath to be to your child what is to you, not because of your training and habits, but because of your own experiences. It should be a day you really love and rejoice in. Let us study the wonderful significance and the rich blessings connected with the Sabbath.

Look upon it as the *day of rest,* of entering into

God's own wonderful rest. The rest of God is in a finished work. By faith in that work we enter into that rest, and the great calm, the peace that passes understanding, keeps the heart and mind. (See Genesis 2:3 and Hebrews 4:3-10.)

Look upon it as a *holy day,* the day God has given us a pledge that He who is holy makes us holy, too. (See Exodus 31:13 and Ezekiel 20:12.) It is in fellowship with God that we are made holy. Let His presence, His love, and His joy be the mark as well as the fruit of keeping it holy.

Look upon it as a *day of blessing.* (See Genesis 2:3.) The Sabbath is the blessing God gave on the day sin robbed us. In the resurrection of Christ, the finished work of creation was restored, finished, and perfected in a higher sense. After the resurrection of Jesus Christ, the first day of the week became the Sabbath of the new life. It took the place of the Sabbath of death, when the Lord of the Sabbath was in the tomb. The Sabbath of creation, rendered void by the fall and the law, is now glorified in the Sabbath of redemption.

Now all the blessings of the Living Christ, His finished work and resurrection power and eternal rest, are to be made ours by this day. Let it be to you a day of blessing, in the fellowship of the Father's love, and the Son's grace, through the Holy Spirit. Then, you will have taken the first and the surest step for its also being a blessing and a joy to your son and your daughter.

The Children Must Keep The Sabbath

Now comes the second lesson. It is not enough that the parents keep the Sabbath day. He must make sure his child does, too. It is not enough that Christian parents seek to keep the day holy themselves. The training of their children to do the same is a sacred obligation placed upon them. This duty requires the sacrifice of personal enjoyment, the exercise of thought and wisdom, and the patience of much faith and love.

In seeking to fulfill this duty, there are two dangers to be avoided. In human nature we find that there are two principles implanted in our hearts to guide us to action—*pleasure* and *duty*.

Pleasure leads us to seek what is agreeable and for our own interest. It is one of the most powerful motives in all our conduct. When our pleasure, however, is at variance with the interests of others or the will of God, the sense of *duty* comes in to restrain and regulate the desire for pleasure. The reward of obedience to duty is that, in course of time, it is no longer a hindrance to pleasure, but becomes itself the highest pleasure. The art of education is to bring pleasure and duty into harmony. Both may be attained without the sacrifice of either.

The Duty Of Keeping The Sabbath

Do not hesitate to speak of God's command and of duty. Education involves in its first stages, more the training of good habits than the teaching of principles—these come later. Do not hesitate to encourage self-denial and quiet self-control which obedience to God's will and to your will brings over the child's spirit. They are part of the foundation of noble character. Tranquility of mind and serenity of spirit are invaluable blessings which the quiet of the Sabbath helps to foster.

Holiness is much more than separation—it is a positive fellowship and enjoyment of God. However, holiness begins with separation: the putting away of week-day toys and books and companions. The marking off of the Sabbath from other days, even in little things, is, under wise guidance, preparation for truly reverencing it later on in life.

The Pleasure Of Keeping The Sabbath

On the other hand, the parent should think of wise and loving ways to make the day a happy one. This can be done by providing Bible stories for the younger ones and carefully selecting suitable and interesting reading for the older ones. A portion of the day can be spent singing psalms and hymns and spiritual songs, making melody to the Lord. Children should be encouraged to spend time in personal Bible study and prayer. The believing parent will find ways of bringing the child to call the Sabbath a delight, the holy of the Lord. Then they can inherit the blessing promised in Isaiah 58:13,14.

Dear Christian parents, the thought of how we ought to train our children to love the Sabbath reminds us of our own shortcomings. Do not be discouraged. We have God, the God of the Sabbath. He will teach us and our children to sanctify His day. Let us look to Him to give us grace to feel and show that the Lord's day is the happiest day of the week. In the divided life of the ordinary, worldly Christian, it cannot be so. God's commandments cannot be obeyed without a whole-hearted surrender to live for Him alone under the full power of His Holy Spirit. If God is our greatest joy and we desire and love to serve Him, He Himself will sanctify our Sabbaths, our hearts, our homes, our children, by His Holy Presence. The Sabbath will become a part of a life holy to the Lord.

A Parent's Prayer

Most Holy God, I thank You for the precious gift of the holy Sabbath day. May each Sabbath lead me deeper into Your rest, the rest of God in Christ, and into the fellowship of Your holiness and Your joy. Blessed Father, I especially ask for grace to train my children to love and honor Your day. Give me wisdom to bring to them the sense of Your holy will and Your loving kindness, in claiming the day for Yourself. May the fear of grieving You and the joy of pleasing You find its rightful place in their hearts. So may the command and the promise, the duty and the pleasure, be one to them. May their delight in Your day meet the promised reward, "Then shalt thou delight thyself in the Lord." Amen.

Chapter 13

THE CHILDREN'S COMMANDMENT

"Honor thy father and thy mother that thy days may be long upon the land which the Lord thy God giveth thee"—Exodus 20:12.

"Children, obey your parents in the Lord: for this is right" —Ephesians 6:1.

"Children, obey your parents in all things: for this is well pleasing unto the Lord"—Colossians 3:20.

In the Ten Commandments, the first four commandments have reference to God, and the last five to our neighbor. In between stands the fifth commandment. It is linked to the first four, because to the young child the parent takes the place of God. From the parent the child must learn to trust and obey his God. The fifth commandment is the transition to the last five, because the family is the foundation of society. As the training school for all our relationships with God and man, this commandment lies at the foundation of all divine and human law.

Of the ten, this one is especially the children's

commandment. For this reason it is especially the parents' commandment. A wise ruler makes good subjects and a firm commander forms faithful soldiers. The children's fulfillment of this precept depends on the parent's character. This leads us to consider what parents must be like if they are to succeed in training their children to honor them.

The Sentiment Of Honor

The sentiment of honor is one of the noblest and purest of our nature. Nothing brings truer honor than giving honor to others. This attitude ought to be cultivated most carefully in the child, as an important part of his education. It is one of the chief elements of a noble character, and prepares the child for rendering to God the honor due to Him.

Scripture teaches us to honor God, to honor all men, to honor the widows, to give honor to whom honor is due. If these principles are to be obeyed by our children, they must prepare for it by learning first to honor their parents. If they are to honor God, they must begin by honoring their parents. In later life they must honor all men by recognizing, even in the most lowly and lost person, the worth that belongs to them as created in the image of God. To do this they must be carefully prepared for it in the school of family life.

Learning to honor others creates a pleasant home atmosphere and puts the relationship of parent and child in its proper perspective. It also prepares the child for all his future relationships to God and his fellow-men. Honoring others is one of the foundation stones of a noble character and a holy life. Parents should study how they can train their children to fulfill this commandment.

Honor Creates Obedience

The child must honor the parent in obedience. *"Obey* your parents" is the New Testament version of "Honour thy father and thy mother." The importance of this word, obedience, is more than the mind can grasp. God created a man, with his wonderful liberty of will, that he might obey Him. Obedience to God was given to lead to the enjoyment of God. By disobedience sin entered but in obedience salvation comes. It comes through the twofold obedience, of Christ and to Christ. (See Hebrews 5:8,9.)

The responsibility of training the child to obey is given to the parent. All memories of happiness and love in the child's home life must be linked with obedience. The parent can do this by working this principle into the child's mind and heart, not so much by instruction or reasoning, as by training and securing the habit of obedience.

Mastering The Will Of The Child

The child is to be taught to honor the parent. The will of the child, his mind and affections, are given into the parent's hands to mold and guide. It is in yielding his will to the will of the parent that the child acquires mastery over his own will and over himself. This mastery will later be his

81

strength and security, making him a fit instrument for doing God's will. Man was created free that he might obey. Obedience is the path to liberty.

On this point parents often make mistakes. They often say that to develop the will of the child the will must be left free, and the child must be left to decide for himself. They forget that the will of the child is not free. Passion and prejudice, selfishness and ignorance, seek to influence the child in the wrong direction. The parent with his superior judgment and experience must make decisions for the child because his will has been entrusted to the parent's care.

Are we not in danger of repressing the healthy development of a child's moral powers by demanding submission to our will? Not at all. The true liberty of the will consists in our being master of it, and so we are our own masters. Train a child to master his will by giving it up to his parent's command, and he acquires the mastery to use it when he is free. Yielding to a parent's control is the path to self-control, and self-control alone is liberty.

The child who is taught by a wise parent to honor him and his superior wisdom will acquire, as he gives up his own way, the power over his will. He is much different from the child who is taught to think that the parent must first convince him to do a particular thing and then obtain his consent before he will do it. The New Testament says very distinctly, "Children, obey your parents in the Lord: for *this is right.*" This is the true reason for its being obeyed—not because the child approves or agrees, but because the command is given by a parent. In obedience, the parent is to be honored.

Developing Manners In Children

In all his attitudes and conduct, the child is to be trained to honor the parent. Familiarity breeds contempt. In language and behavior, parents often tolerate an easygoing familiarity, which is mistakenly called love or kindness. This attitude destroys respect and reverence in which true love has its strength and its real happiness. Manners are of more importance than many people think. The neglect of good manners not only reveals a lack of respect and courtesy, but it fosters selfishness and indifference that show little concern for the feelings of others. Manners are the most important thing in education, more so than learning.

Let parents remember that by training their children to show honor and respect, even in insignificant things, they are forming habits in them which will afterward repay all their labor. "Them that honour Me I will honour" is God's law (1 Samuel 2:30). This also has its reflection in the life of earth. None have received higher honor on earth than those who have learned to honor all men, to honor the poor and needy.

Developing Honor In Children

It is the parent who is to cultivate and develop this attitude in the child. The young child is guided, not by disapproval or argument, but by feeling and affection. He cannot yet realize and honor the unseen God. He cannot yet honor the unlovely and unworthy or see the value of their creation in God's image. The child can only honor what he sees to be "worthy of honor."

This is the parent's high calling: and to speak, to act, and to live in the child's presence in such a way that honor may be spontaneously communicated. This can only happen when the parent lives in God's presence, and walks worthy of this calling, as one who has been placed at the head of a family, to be not only its prophet, priest, but king, too. Yes, a king receives honor. Therefore, let the parent as a king rule and reign in love and the fear of God, and his honor will be given him.

Above all, let parents remember that honor really comes from God. Let them honor Him in the eyes of their children, and He will honor them there, too. Let them beware of honoring their children more than God. This is the surest way to grief for parents and children together. Children will learn to honor God and their parents when they see their parents honoring God in everything they do. The parent who teaches his child to obey the fifth commandment has guided his feet into the way of *all* God's commandments. A child's first virtue is the honoring and obeying of his parents.

A Parent's Prayer

Lord God, fill my own soul with such honor and reverence for Your holy majesty that both I and my child may learn what honor is. Teach me to claim honor from my child with the holy aim of leading him to honor You above all. May honoring his parents and honoring his God create in my child the spirit of humility. May I be kept from the terrible sin of ever honoring my child more than my God. Lord, I look to You for grace to secure the keeping of this, the children's commandment in my home. May the training of young souls to keep Your commandments, to honor and serve You, be the fruit of Your own Spirit's work in me. I ask in Jesus' name. Amen.

Chapter 14

INSTRUCTING YOUR CHILDREN

"These are the commandments. . .which the Lord your God commanded to teach you. . .that thou mightest fear the Lord thy God, to keep all His statutes and His commandments, which I command thee, thou, and thy son, and thy son's son, all the days of thy life. . .Thou shalt love the Lord thy God with all thine heart. . .And these words, which I command thee this day, shall be in thine heart. . .And thou shalt teach them diligently unto thy children, and shalt talk of them when thou sittest in thine house, and when thou walkest by the way, and when thou liest down, and when thou risest up." — Deuteronomy 6:1,2,5-7

"Thou, and thy son, and thy son's son," with these words Moses gave expression to the thought that God's purpose in giving His commandments to His people was not limited to the individual or to a single generation. God had all the people in mind, throughout all generations. This purpose of God has to be the law of individual duty. Each one who received the commandments of God was to strive not only to keep them himself, but to hold himself responsible for their observance among his children.

"These are the commandments which the Lord your God commanded to teach you. . .that thou mightest fear the Lord thy God, to keep all His commandments. . .thou and thy son, and thy son's son" (Deuteronomy 6:1,2). The duty of the parents is once again explained. They were to relate to their children the faithfulness of God that had redeemed them from the land of Egypt. This teaches us that the fear and faith of God must be seen in family religion. It was the parent's duty to teach and promote the fear of God in his home.

Instruct With All Your Heart

Parental instruction must come *from the heart*. We all know that instruction has little influence on children when given by an apathetic teacher. It is only the heart that captures the heart of another. It is the loving warmth of interest and affection of the teacher that awakens corresponding emotions in the heart of the pupil. God desires to use all the influence of parental love to gain access for His words and His will into the youthful hearts of the children of His people. God's Word says, "Thou shalt love the Lord thy God *with all thine heart,* and these words. . .shall be in thine heart. . .and thou shalt teach them diligently unto thy children."

How easy and how blessed is the work of those who listen to God's guidance. It is your duty and your joy to love the Lord your God with all your heart. If you love Him, then love His words, too. Let them live in your heart and let them have a place in your affections. When the heart is filled with God's love and God's Word, it is easy to have them in your mouth, too, and to teach them to your children. Let holy love for God and His words mingle with your tender love for your little ones. It will be a sweet and happy work to win your beloved on earth to the Father beloved in heaven.

When the work of instructing the children becomes a burden, you may be sure it is an indication of something wrong within your own heart. Your love for God in heaven, or the delight in His Word, has been fading. When you need more energy to joyfully perform your work, you must only turn to the words that reveal the secret of a godly education. Then, you will experience an unspeakable blessing in the wisdom that connects the heart's secret love with the mouth's spoken words: "Thou shalt love the Lord thy God *with all thy heart*. And these words shall be *in thy heart*. And thou shalt teach them to thy children." We must remember that this is the divinely appointed ministry for the salvation of our children—parental love elevated and strengthened by the love of God, guided and inspired by His own Holy Word.

Instruct With Diligence

Parental instruction must also be diligent and earnest: "Thou shalt *diligently* teach them unto thy children"—or, as it reads in the original Hebrew, "Thou shalt sharpen them unto thy children." The word is used of the sharpening of weapons, as arrows and spears, to make them penetrate deeply. We must not communicate a cold declaration of His will or mere intellectual knowledge. The arrow shot from the bow has little effect unless it has been sharpened—to pierce the heart of the enemy. In the same way, the godly parent must use diligence to consider how he can best penetrate his child's heart with the words that he speaks.

He must carefully consider how he can best gain both the child's understanding and affections. He does this by making the most of opportunities and activities in which the child is interested. The parent must also learn the art of speaking in the spirit of love. His whole life must be an attractive example of what he has taught. There is nothing that drives home the word of instruction like a consistent and holy life.

Above all, the parent must wait for the Holy Spirit who alone can make the word sharp as a two-edged sword. Then the parent will come to experience the truth of these words: "The words of the wise are as. . .nails fastened by the masters of assemblies, which are given from one shepherd" (Ecclesiastes 12:11). God's promise is sure:

the blessing of the Spirit will not be withheld from those who make an earnest and prayerful effort.

Instruct With Perseverance

Parental instruction must be *persevering* and continuous. "Thou shalt teach them diligently unto thy children, and shalt talk of them when thou sittest in thine house, and when thou walkest by the way, and when thou liest down, and when thou risest up." The entrance of divine truth into the mind and heart, the formation of habit and the training of character, are not attained by sudden and isolated efforts, but by regular and unceasing repetition. This is the law of all growth in nature, and God seeks to make use of this law in His Kingdom.

This is the principle that is so beautifully applied by Moses to parental duty. The parental instruction he required was not to be at set times, and stated in formal lectures. The whole life with all its duties has to be interwoven with the lessons of God's presence and God's service. With a heart full of God's love and God's Word, the ordinary activities of daily life help to lead youthful hearts toward heaven.

You can instruct your child while sitting in the home, or walking together, or in duties of the day. Relaxing at home or talking around the dinner table provides opportunities for recognizing the goodness and rejoicing in the service of the ever-present One. From early morning to evening rest—the whole day provides occasion for uninterrupted fellowship with the Holy One. Every activity can be used to point the little ones to the unseen and ever-near Father in heaven.

The objection could be made that all this speaking would tire and alienate the child. Parents will receive wisdom from on high and be guided to know when and how to speak to their children. Love will influence their children's hearts and find a willing and listening ear when others would only grow weary!

A Parent's Prayer

Blessed God, give me wisdom and grace to be the teacher of my children that You would have me to be. I see how You do not permit any other to assume the parent's position. You have appointed me the first and most important teacher. Fill our hearts with Your love and Your Word. Help us to sharpen Your words deep into our children's hearts. Help us all day long to walk in Your love and presence, and influence our children for You. Amen.

Chapter 15

A CHRISTIAN HOME

"As for me and my house, we will serve the Lord"—Joshua 24:15.

In God's dealing with Noah and Abraham, and with Israel in the Passover and at Mount Sinai, we have repeatedly noticed the deep meaning of the united mention of father and children in His commands and promises. "Thou *and* thy house," "thou *and* thy seed," "ye *and* your children," "thou *and* thy son." Such is the language of the covenant God. In the words of Joshua we have the response from earth, "as for me *and* my house." The divine principle is clear: the parent accepts God's promises for his family as well as for himself. The covenant undertaking of the Father in heaven is met by the covenant obligation of the father on earth. Joshua is to us the model of a godly parent. In him we can see how to fulfill our parental responsibilities.

Consecrate Yourself

Joshua began with himself. "As for *me* and my

house." We cannot too strongly express the truth that for godly training the first and the most essential requirement is personal consecration. It is good to reflect on our responsibility, to speak with our children, and to pray for them—but all these are only accessories. The first thing on the part of the parent is a life devoted to God and His service. It is this that creates the spiritual atmosphere the children are to breathe. It is this that gives our performance of duty and our dealings with our children their spiritual influence. It is this that gives our praying and our working its value with God.

"As for me," there must be no hesitation or half-heartedness in our confession of devotion to God's service. As often as the prayer for God's blessing on the children comes up, it must be in the spirit of David: "Therefore now let it please Thee to bless the house of Thy servant" (1 Chronicles 17:27). With God and men, in the home and out of it, as well as in the hearts of parents themselves, it must be a settled thing: "As for me, I will serve the Lord."

Consecrate Your Family

Take your stand for all who belong to you: "As for me, *and my house, we* will serve the Lord." There are religious parents who do not understand that this is their duty and their privilege. They do not understand what God has put in their power. They imagine they honor God by thinking that the religion of their children is dependent on God's will apart from their involvement as parents. They are so occupied, either with the activities of this life or with religious work, that they cannot find the time for speaking and acting out the grand decision: "As for me and my house, *we will* serve the Lord."

Perhaps, the father leaves the religion of the children to the care of the mother, and the mother thinks that the father as head is more responsible. They hesitate or neglect to come to a clear and definite understanding, and the spiritual education of their children does not take the prominent place it ought to be in the parent's relationship.

Let each believing parent receive Joshua's words, first, in the depth of his own soul, then in fellowship with marriage partner and children. In our prayers and conversations, we must say that our house is holy to the Lord. Our children must be trained first of all for God and His service. The more we express this belief, the more this principle will assert itself and help us to guide our household to serve the Lord, too.

Serve The Lord

The words of Joshua teach us that our consecration to God must be practical: "We will serve the Lord." There are many parents who view Christianity only in terms of salvation, and not in terms of service. They pray most earnestly that all their children may be saved. If their children spend their lives in the service of the world, they comfort themselves with the idea that they will yet be saved before they die. No wonder that their training for this life has been a failure. These parents never understood the truth and never trained their children to understand that to train for God's service secures the fullest salvation.

God said to Abraham, "I know him that he will command his children and his household after him, that they shall keep the way of the Lord. . .that the Lord may bring upon Abraham that which He hath spoken of him" (Genesis 18:19). Remember God's words in connection with Israel's deliverance from Egypt: "Let My people go that they may *serve* Me." Remember Pharaoh's reply, "Go ye, *serve* the Lord. . .let your little ones also go with you" (Exodus 10:24). The Holy Spirit has spoken, "How much more shall the blood of Christ. . .purge your conscience from dead works to *serve* the living God" (Hebrews 9:14).

All redemption is for service. God does not want to be worshipped without being served. The glory of heaven will be that "His servants shall serve Him" (Revelation 22:3). Let our lives and our homes be consecrated to serving God. Let obeying His will, carrying out His commands, doing His work, and devoting ourselves to the interests of His Kingdom give family life its proper place of importance.

Confess Your Decision

It was in the presence of tens of thousands of the children of Israel that Joshua made his bold confession, "Choose you this day whom ye will

95

serve. . .as for me and my house, we will serve the Lord." His was not to be the religion of the nation or the religion of neighbors. Everyone else could reject God, and he be left alone, but still the Lord Jehovah would be his God. Just as Abraham had to leave his father's house, and Israel had to leave Egypt, Joshua, too, had to be a man of decision and confession. He had to come out and be separate— one of a peculiar people unto the Lord. This is the kind of consecration we want in our family life, where God's own holy and blessed will is revealed to us by the Holy Spirit.

How often parents, whose early married life was marked by decision and earnestness, later become aware of spiritual coldness in their lives because they give in to the demands of their children or their friends. It may seem difficult to be peculiar. Yet, if we trust God for His guidance, and yield ourselves to His personal friendship, the joy of separation from the world will be abundant for ourselves and our children.

Unite Your Family

If this page is read by parents who are aware that their own and their family's service of God has not been as God would have it, let me give a word of advice. Father and mother must discuss this matter with one another. Say what you have often felt, but each has kept to himself. Say that it is your united desire to live as entirely for God as grace can enable you to do. If your children are old enough, include them, too, and ask if they will join in this holy covenant, "We will serve the Lord."

Let this covenant from time to time be renewed in a distinct act of consecration, that the conviction may be confirmed: We do want to be a holy family, a house where God dwells. Ours must be a home completely consecrated to God. Do not worry that you will be unable to keep this vow. It is not we who have to do the work and then bring it to God. We may count upon Him to accept, confirm, and carry out the purpose of our heart, "As for me and my house, we will serve the Lord."

A Parent's Prayer

Lord God, I thank You for what I have learned from Your servant Joshua in his faithfulness to You as the father in his own home. I humbly ask You to give me grace to say as distinctly and as publicly as he did, "As for me and my house, we will serve the Lord." Lord, I consecrate myself to you. My Father, let Your love for me, and my love for You, be my inspiration and my joy. May my children see that I serve You with my whole heart. Lord, I consecrate my family to you. Help me to train my children to serve You. Remove every inconsistency and all weakness that might hinder anyone in my family from being completely Yours. May mine be a truly consecrated home.

Lord, help us to serve you in practical ways. Let the knowing and the doing of God's will, the working for His Kingdom, the seeking His glory, be the one desire of our hearts. May our home be a blessing to others by encouraging them to take a stand for You. Lord God, let Your Spirit work mightily in the homes of Your people, that everywhere this confession may be heard ringing out: "As for me and my house, we will serve the Lord." Amen.

Chapter 16

COMMITTED CHRISTIAN PARENTS

"And Manoah said, Now let thy words come to pass. How shall we order the child and how shall we do unto him?"—Judges 13:12.

An angel of the Lord appeared to Manoah's wife. He came to predict the birth of a child, who would be a Nazarite unto God and a deliverer of God's people. The first feeling of Manoah on receiving the tidings from his wife was that to train such a God-given child for God's service, God-given grace would be needed. He prayed to the Lord and said, "O my Lord, let the man of God which thou didst send come again unto us, and teach us what we shall do unto the child that shall be born" (Judges 13:8). When in answer to his prayer the angel came again, his one petition was, "How shall we order the child, and how shall we do unto him?" (verse 12). Let us consider the prayer, the answer, and the blessings these parents received.

The Need For Prayer

Notice the deep sense of responsibility Manoah feels for the holy work of training a child as a Nazarite unto God. The angel had already given Manoah's wife the necessary instructions. But Manoah was so deeply impressed with the holiness of their calling as parents of this child, that he asked for the angel to come again and teach them. What a contrast to the careless self-confidence with which many Christian parents today undertake the training of their children.

What would we think of a man offering to manage a bank or to navigate an ocean liner who had no training to equip him to do either? What must be said of the presumption that feels no fear in taking charge of a child's immortal spirit of priceless value, and undertakes to guide it through the temptations and dangers of life? If only all Christian parents would learn from Manoah to feel and confess their ignorance, and, like him, to set themselves at once to seek and obtain the grace he needs.

We note, further, how Manoah's sense of need immediately found expression in prayer. He believed in God as the living God, as the hearer of prayer. He believed that when God gave a command or a task, He would also give the grace to do it right. He believed that when God gave a child to be trained for His service, He would also give the wisdom needed to do so. Instead of the sense of unfitness and weakness depressing him, or the sense of his obligation causing him to work in his own strength, he simply prayed. Prayer to Manoah was the solution to difficulties, the supply of need, the source of wisdom and strength.

Each child is a gift of God as truly as Manoah's, and has as much right as his to be trained for God and His service. Like him, we can count most confidently upon the Father, who has entrusted the child to us, to give us the grace to train him. Let us only pray, pray believingly, pray without ceasing, at each phase of our task. We can depend upon the fact that God hears the prayers of a parent seeking wisdom to train his child.

There is one thing more we must especially observe in regard to Manoah's prayer. He prayed after his wife had told him of the angel's instructions. Manoah longed to hear them himself, to be sure and certain. As parents, we have in God's Word clear and complete directions as to the training of our children. Our own experience or that of others may have supplied us with much information to help us, but this does not diminish the need for prayer. With each child, we always need renewed wisdom direct from above. Daily renewed prayer is the secret of training our children for God.

God's Answer To Prayer

Manoah's story also teaches us that God loves to answer a parent's cry. The angel had nothing new to communicate beyond what he had previously said to the woman. Yet, God sent the angel because He will not ignore the parent who seeks to fully know His will. The fact of the angel having come once encouraged Manoah to hope he might come a second time. Those who have already had communications with God concerning teaching their children, will be those who desire more instruction.

The answer to Manoah's prayer contained no new revelation. It simply pointed back to the instruction previously given: "Of all that I said unto the woman let her beware. . .all that I commanded her let her observe" (Judges 13:13,14). In answer to our prayer, it may be that no new truth will be revealed, perhaps even no new thought impressed. However, the answer to the prayer may be something better. The Holy Spirit may lead us back to what the Lord has already spoken, to study more carefully the principles laid down in Holy Scripture for the training of our children. It is then that we will realize as never before how our children are the Lord's, and they must be kept holy for Him. We will more deeply understand how parents are God's ministers, in whose holy life the children are to be blessed.

The Christian Parent

The angel had only spoken of the life of the mother before the birth of the child: the Nazarite child must have a Nazarite mother. She was not to eat or drink of the fruit of the vine or eat any unclean thing. Separation from the world to special purity and holiness—this was God's secret of parental duty.

Education involves not so much what we do or say, but most of all *what we are.* This is true not only when our children are of an age to see and judge, but even before their birth. In that holy time of mystery, when mother and child are still one, and influences from a mother's spirit pass into the child, God says, "Of all that I said unto the woman let her beware. . .all that I command her let her observe." This requires a life of moderation and self-denial that does not ask how far and deep it may go into the world to enjoy all that is not absolutely forbidden. Instead, she willingly gives up whatever is not helpful to her consecration and fellowship with God.

It is a life of purity and obedience that is the preparation for a mother's and a father's work. God's answer to the prayer, "How shall we order the child?" is, "As you live, you train." Live as a Nazarite, holy to the Lord, and your child will be a Nazarite unto God, a deliverer of His people Israel.

The Parent's Blessing

The blessing that resulted from Manoah's prayer was something more than the answer. There was the blessed revelation of God Himself, and the wonderful knitting together of the hearts of the parents. The angel of the Lord had revealed himself in such a way that Manoah felt, "We have seen God" (Judges 13:22). When he asked the angel's name, his name was *Wonderful*—"and the angel did *wondrously*." And this is still the name of the parent's God, "*Wonderful*"(verse 19).

Just as Manoah did, we pray, wait for, and accept His divine teaching. He is wonderful in His love, wonderful in His ways, and wonderful in His work. He is wonderful in what He does for us as parents, and wonderful in what He does through us for our children. Let us worship the Lord, the parent's God, whose name is *Wonderful*! Let our prayer, like Manoah's, end in praise and worship, in faith and truth.

How rich was the blessing this revelation brought to the praying couple. What a picture the chapter gives us of the way in which father and mother are lovingly to help each other in all that concerns their children. Manoah's wife gets the message from the angel and immediately tells her husband. He prays at once for more light and fuller teaching. The angel comes again to her, and she runs to tell Manoah, who follows her. He hears again what his wife had been told. When the sacrifice was offered, Manoah and his wife looked on together and together fell on their faces to the ground. When Manoah was afraid and spoke, "We shall surely die because we have seen God," she comforted him and strengthened his faith.

What blessed fellowship of love and faith, of prayer and worship develops between husband and wife because of their child. It is not only parents who are to be a blessing to their children, but children to their parents, too. The parents talk together of God's promises and His commands, and each tells the other what has been revealed to him. They unite in seeking to know and carry out God's will, praying together and then falling down in worship before Him whose name is *Wonderful*. They unburden their fears and encourage each other to trust and hope. In all of this they experience that the home is as much for training parent's themselves as their children. They have learned that nothing opens the fountains of divine love and of each other's love more than the prayerful desire to know how to raise the children God has given them for His service and glory.

A Parent's Prayer

Blessed Lord, as those whom You have joined together to train children for your holy service, we bow in united worship before You. Make us by Your Holy Spirit to be of one heart and mind, so that all You reveal to the one may at once be witnessed to the other. Lord God, we come to You now for wisdom for each child You have given us. Open our eyes to see the treasures of wisdom in Your Holy Word, in promise and instruction for parents and children. Especially reveal Yourself to us as the God of the covenant and the promise, the parent's God, whose name is *Wonderful*. Teach us to walk before You in holy fear and reverence, in childlike trust and joy, in purity of life and separation from the world. Help us to train our children as Nazarites, holy to the Lord, prepared to fight for the Kingdom, and to be the deliverers of the oppressed. Amen.

Chapter 17

YOUR CHILD—GOD'S POSSESSION

"For this child I prayed; and the Lord hath given me my petition which I asked of Him: therefore also I have lent him to the Lord; as long as he liveth he shall be lent to the Lord"—1 Samuel 1:27,28.

The relationship between the believing parent and the Lord in reference to his child has been presented to us in different ways. In Samuel's story we have a new and very beautiful expression of this relationship. Hannah had received her son from the Lord in answer to her prayer. The love and joy of her heart could find no better way of expressing themselves than in giving her child to the Lord again, for as long as he lives. This thought comes into the heart of many a Christian mother as she looks on her firstborn little one. When considered carefully, this thought reveals some of the most precious lessons of parental faith and duty. Whether we think of God, of our child, or of ourselves, there is every reason to say, "As long as he liveth he is given to the Lord."

Your Child Belongs To God

God looks upon my child as His, and he has only been loaned to me to train. The child is indeed not mine but the Lord's. Because I am naturally inclined to forget this, I love and treat the child as if he were altogether mine. For this reason, it is such a precious privilege to give him to the Lord for all the days of his life.

God has not only a right to the child, but He needs him. The work He has to do upon earth is so great, and He has so planned the work for each person, that He would not leave out even one of His children. I have so often heard of a mother joyfully sacrificing an only son, or all her sons, for her king or country. I consider it an even greater honor to give to my King the child who is His, and whom He has loaned me, with the privilege of loving and training and enjoying him. I love my Lord and have often asked what I can render to Him for His love to me. I delight to give what is my most precious possession upon earth to be His. To Him who gave His Son for me, to Him alone, all I am and have belongs. My child, too, I have given to the Lord as long as he shall live.

Your Child Needs God

It is not only for God's sake, but for my child's sake that I give him to the Lord. The more I love my child, the more heartily I give him away to God. Nowhere can he be safe or happy except with Him. I do love my precious little one, and yet how little I can do for him! I know he is born in sin and has inherited from me an evil nature, which no care or love of mine can overcome. If I give my child to God I know that He accepts him and takes him for His own. God will make my child one with His beloved Son, cleansing him in the precious blood. In a second birth by His Spirit, God will give him a new nature. He, the great God, will adopt my child as His, and take him up to His own home for all eternity.

He will use me as His minister, giving me all the wisdom I need to properly train my child as His. Do not ask me why I give my child to God! It is because I love my child. Who would not give their child to such a God, for such blessings?

The Parent's Double Blessing

For my own sake, too, I give my child to the Lord, because—and this is so wonderful—the child I give to God becomes doubly my own. The child I give to God, He holds for me and then gives him back again. I then possess my child without the fear of sinning in loving him as my own and without the fear of ever losing him.

Even if death were to come and take him from me here, I would know that he was still mine in the Father's home. He was only taken from me for a time to serve in the King's own palace. God gave him to me and I gave my precious child back to Him. God gave him once again to me, and once again I gave him back to God. Giving my child has become the link of a most blessed friendship and relationship between God and me.

If He leaves my child with me on earth, having given my dear one to Him, I am confident that all the grace and wisdom I need for training him will be given. I need not worry because my child is now the Lord's. Will He not provide for all His child needs? If the parent wants to know how to love and enjoy and train his child in the right way, let him give the child to God.

These are some of the blessed reasons a parent gives his child to God. Let us now consider how this consecration of the child is to be maintained and carried out in his training at home.

Praying For The Child

Let the parent use his consecration of the child as a plea with God in prayer. The grace promised for training a child is not given at once, but day by day. In the training of our children, difficulties will often arise in which it seems as if God's help does not come. Then, it is time for prayer and faith. The power of sin may manifest itself in the child's natural character. There may at times be more characteristics to create fear than hope. Our own ignorance, or unfaithfulness, or weakness may often make us fear that we may be the cause of our child's not growing up as the Lord's. At such times, as at all times, God must be our refuge.

Let us then maintain our consecration of the child and pray for him. We gave him to the Lord and we refuse to take him back because either we, or the child, are guilty. We plead for grace for the child who has been given by us and accepted by God. The child is His now, and we can leave him with God. Such faith will give rest and bring a sure blessing.

Reasoning With The Child

Let the child know, even if we do not often say so in words, that he has been given to God. Let him know that this is the reason we cannot give way to his will or allow sin in him—we must keep him for God. Let the child know, with gentleness and firmness, that this is not just an empty declaration, but a principle that motivates us. Let him realize this so that it will gradually become a motive within himself. Because he has been given to God and accepted by Him, how could he disobey or grieve Him? Let our words, our life, our prayer and education, make the child feel, "I am the Lord's."

Training The Child

Since we have given our child to the Lord, let us use this act of consecration as a motive to faithfully discharge our duties. We easily become distracted by the pressing business of life and the spirit of the world all around us. Consecrated training requires complete devotion in daily life. Let us look at our children in the light of this great transaction with God—I have given my child to the Lord. This reminder can stir us to greater diligence, to faith, and to prayer.

Let us especially act under the influence of this motive as we think of the profession for which we are educating our child. *God needs servants for His temple.* Let us ask Him what place He has for each child in His Kingdom. If this thought motivated each parent who has given his child to God, a far greater number of young Christians would grow up to work for God. If all the children whose parents profess to have consecrated them to God were really brought up that way, we would have no shortage of believers to take their place in the service of God. We need more consecrated parents like Hannah and more children receiving a consecrated education like Samuel's. May God by His Holy Spirit teach us the full meaning and power of the words we use! "I have given my child to be the Lord's as long as he lives."

A Parent's Prayer

My Father, this child is now Yours—and mine! My soul is humbled at the thought of this great privilege, this joint ownership of my child between God and me. I look to You for the grace to enable me to keep this treasure which is to be given back to You. Teach me to love my child with a holy love and to train him for the service of Your temple. Teach me to speak to him about You and Your love so that his heart may early be won for You. May my whole life be an inspiration to my child to help him to see what is pure, lovely, and pleasing to You. Cause my child early to hear the voice that called Samuel, and in childlike simplicity and reverence to answer, "Speak, Lord, Thy servant heareth." Amen.

Chapter 18

WHY PARENTS FAIL

"(Thou) honourest thy sons above me. . .for them that honour Me I will honour, and they that despise me shall be lightly esteemed"—Samuel 2:29,30.

"I will judge his house for ever for the iniquity which he knoweth; because his sons made themselves vile, and he restrained them not" —1 Samuel 3:13.

Some men are born to rule. It is their very nature, and they often do it instinctively. There are others to whom it never comes naturally. They either withdraw from it; or, if they attempt it, they utterly fail. They appear to be lacking in the gifts that equip them for this work of governing others. It is always a struggle and an effort for them. In ordinary life men can choose, or are chosen for, the situations they have to fill as rulers or commanders. In family life we have a very unusual and very serious situation: Every parent has to rule, whether he is suited for it or not. The fact that he is not suited does not take away his responsibility.

The terrible consequences of his failure to rule still have an effect upon him and his children.

Feeble old Eli was faithful to God's cause and ready to die for the sacred ark of God, but he was unfaithful to his duty as a parent. He failed to restrain his sons. Let us study the causes, the consequences, and the cure for this parental failure.

Causes Of Parental Failure

We have said that one of the reasons parents fail to rule is that they lack natural ability. However, this is never so absolute that determined effort could not remedy this weakness, or that the grace of God could not change it. We must, therefore, look for other causes.

The chief cause of parental failure is the *lack of self-discipline.* A Christian must not ask if a task is easy or natural, if he likes it, or if it appears possible. His question must be: What is duty? What has God commanded? There is wonderful strengthening, even for the weakest character, in giving oneself to the divine *ought* and *must* of God's will. The fear of grieving the Father, the desire of pleasing Him, the assurance of His strength to aid our weakness—such thoughts activate the energies of the soul. Nothing is so invigorationg as the hearty effort to obey.

Most Christian parents do not realize and are not taught by the Church, that ruling the home well is a simple matter of duty. Because many parents do not recognize this as a God-given command that must be obeyed, many children are spoiled and ruined. Not to restrain the child is to dishonor God by honoring the child more than God. This good-natured weakness is mistakenly called kindness, because it cannot bear to reprimand, to restrain, or to punish a child.

Another cause of parental weakness is *laziness*. The parent does not take the trouble to rule and guide his feelings by God's Word. He refuses the pain which punishing the child causes him. The lazy parent does not realize that he is choosing the greater pain of seeing his child grow up unrestrained. No grace of the Christian life is obtained without sacrifice. The task of influencing and forming other souls for God needs special self-sacrifice. Like every difficult work, it needs purpose, attention, perseverance.

The greatest cause for parental failure is a *spiritual problem*. It is the lack of true devotion to God Himself. Because God is the great ruler and educator, the parent's authority is ordained by God. The parent who does not live under command to God in his own life, does not have the secret of authority and command over others. The fear of God is the beginning of wisdom—this also applies to the work of ruling. It is failure in personal godliness that is the root of parental failure.

Consequences Of Parental Failure

There is one element in the law of consequences that is especially serious and dreadful. It is that consequences are not experienced until it is too late to rectify them. Our actions are seeds.

No one who looks at the little seed could ever imagine what a great tree or what bitter fruit could come from it. Consequences, as seen in those around us, somehow hardly affect us. Self-interest flatters itself with the pleasing hope that, in our case at least, the result will not be so disastrous.

When you have been guilty of consulting the will of your children more than the honor of God, look at the picture of Eli and his home under God's judgment. Ponder carefully what God says. Remember that throughout the universe there is no feeling of well-being unless you are in harmony with the law of God. In earth and heaven, in nature and grace, in the individual, the family, and the Church, obedience to the law of God is the only possible path to happiness.

To disobey God's law is to invite disaster. If the parents give way to weakness because of ignorance or laziness, they must expect the natural results. These may not always become manifest in the same degree or with equal speed. However, the result will become evident in the parent's loss of ability to mold their child's character, in the loss of peace and happiness, and in many cases in the loss of the soul forever. These parents must reap what they sow. God appointed parental rule in the family, as the symbol of His own authority, in which parents and children alike are to honor Him. To dishonor Him is to lose His favor and blessing.

The Cure For Parental Failure

In speaking of the causes, we have already indicated some of the solutions. The first solution is this: *determine to do God's will*. My duty is never measured by what I feel is within my power to do, but by what God's grace makes possible for me. I do not know how much grace can enable me to do, until I begin. It is only little by little that the bad habits of laziness and disobedience will be conquered.

Let the weak parent accept this as his God-imposed duty: he must *rule his children*. Let him remember that not to rule and restrain his children means that both parent and child dishonor God by not doing His will. Let him yield himself to the God of grace, with the purpose to do His will, however impossible it may appear. The surrender will be accepted, and the grace not withheld. Step by step, along with many failures, the honest effort to do God's will cannot remain without its reward.

Next to this, let the parent who has failed, study some of the simplest laws in the art of ruling. Like any other skill of which we are ignorant, ruling must be learned. First, *do not give too many commands at once*—begin with only one. If you secure obedience to one, then your own and the child's recognition of your power to rule is established. *Do not command what you cannot enforce,* or what the child does not have the ability to obey. Begin to prove your authority when it is easy for you to secure obedience and when it is easy for the child to render it. As in all learning we must proceed from the easy to the more difficult. *Let your command be given in quiet, deliberate tones,* with full self-control. Hasty or untimely commands lead to disobedience. *Self-rule* is the secret of all rule. As you honor God's law yourself in self-command, others learn to honor it, too.

Above all, let the Christian parent who would rule well, remember God. You are God's minister, doing God's work. God loves the children and wants them trained for Himself. He is your covenant-God and you can depend upon Him to be your help and strength. It is God who, through you, will rule your home. Yield yourself to Him. Pray not only for help, but believe most certainly that it is given. Act with the assurance that God's help is given and is beginning, little by little, to work in you. Say to your Father that you desire to do your duty at any risk and to honor Him with your children. In quiet, restful assurance, believe that God's strength will work for you in your weakness.

A Parent's Prayer

Lord, God I understand that if we do not rule and restrain our children, but give them their own way, we honor them more than You. Even before we think of it, weakness can become wickedness in ourselves and our children. Let the thought of Your command to rule our home motivate us with our whole heart to fulfill our holy calling as parents. Let us believe that, as we and our children fulfill Your will, we are in the path of true blessing for this life and the life to come. Amen.

Chapter 19

THE PARENT AS INTERCESSOR

"And it was so, when the days of their feasting were gone about, that Job sent and sanctified them, and rose up early in the morning and offered burnt offerings according to the number of them all: for Job said, It may be that my sons have sinned, and cursed God in their hearts. Thus did Job continually"—Job 1:5.

Job is a beautiful picture of a man in whose heart the fear of God lives! He fears that his children will sin against God or forsake Him in their heart. He is so deeply aware of their sinful nature, the very thought of their having been in circumstances of temptation makes him afraid. He so fully realizes his position and privilege as a father that he sends for them to sanctify them, and takes upon himself the continual offering of the needed sacrifice.

Job is another example of one of God's servants whose fear of God extends to the sin of his children. Even God said of him, "There is none like (my servant Job) in the earth, a perfect and an upright man, one that feareth God, and escheweth evil" (Job 2:3). Job was a man of patience, faith, and holiness. From studying his life we learn that a man's entire consecration to God implies the consecration of the home life, too. Let us study the lessons his example teaches us concerning what it means to be a godly parent.

The Sinful Nature

One of the marks of a godly parent is a deep sense of the sinfulness and the sins of his children. God entered into the parental covenant with Abraham to conquer and free man from sin. Later, the blood of the lamb was sprinkled in the passover to deliver from the cause of sin. Parents were made the instructors of their children to lead them from sin into the service of God.

In all God's dealings with us in redemption and grace, in His revelation in Christ and His cross, He has one goal—to save us from sin and make us partakers of His holiness. If the parent is to be God's fellow-worker, and the blessing promised to him is to come true, the parent himself must be in harmony with God. He must hate sin with a perfect hatred and seek above everything to remove and keep it out of his home.

Let parents ask God to give them a right sense of what sin is in their children, in its curse, its dishonor to God, and its power. Let us ask Him to work in us a very deep conviction so that as His ministers to the children, sin may be removed from them and the power of Christ's victory over sin may be seen in them. His desire is that we, our children, and our home be holy to the Lord.

The Dangers Of Temptation

The natural result of such fear of sin is that parents become very watchful of their children during times of special temptation. Job knew that at a time of feasting there would be special danger. When the days of feasting were over, he sent for his sons and sanctified them. What an impression these children must have received of the fear of sin in their God-fearing father. It must have made them aware of their own need to be watchful of sin and to fear God.

Every careful parent knows there are times and places when the temptations of sin come more quickly and easily surprise even the sweetest child. Before and after a child goes into the company and the circumstances where he may be tempted, a praying father and mother should do what Job did. He sent for his sons and sanctified them.

Let us ask God to make us very watchful and very wise in making use of opportunities to speak to our children about sin. There are times when the child's conscience is especially sensitive, and a word spoken at the right time will sink deep into his heart. There are times when his conscience has been weakened, and a word of prayer will help to wake it up and restore its authority. A parent who is in sympathy with God's purpose to destroy sin, and who puts himself at God's disposal, will be guided as to when and how to speak. This parent will be able to arouse and strengthen in the child the reality of sin and its danger.

Intercede For Your Children

A godly parent has power with God to intercede for his children. Job not only sent for his children to speak to them, but he sanctified them through the burnt offerings he offered. The parent who has accepted the sign of the sprinkling of the blood for his child, and who has sprinkled the blood on the doorposts of his home, has a right to plead that blood with God. His faith obtains pardon for the child. He has a right to intercede for the grace that can save and sanctify.

Through the whole course of God's dealing with parents, from Noah onward, we have seen that God gives the parent the right to act on behalf of the child. All the influence a parent is to exert depends on his being clear on this point: I am the steward of God's grace to the child, and I am heard on his behalf. This makes him confident in saying, I represent God with my child. I have God's help to give me influence and power. I have overcome the power of my child's sin in pleading with God for him, and I am sure of conquering it in pleading with my child.

A Parent's Prayer

Gracious God, I humbly ask You to imprint deep on my heart the lessons Your Holy Word teaches us. May Job be to all parents a lesson and a model of the God-fearing parent. Teach us to tremble at the sins of our children, and intercede for them. Teach us, Lord, to fear sin as the one thing Your soul hates. Make it our main concern to keep our children free from sin. Teach us to realize our God-given position as intercessors and to plead the blood for them with as much faith and assurance as we do for ourselves. May we know in faith that we are heard. Teach us to speak and pray at the right time and in the proper way. May they learn from us both the fear of God and the confidence of faith. Lord God, may our holiness and our faith influence our families and make them completely Yours. Amen.

Chapter 20

RAISING A GOOD CHILD

"Come, ye children, hearken unto me: I will teach you the fear of the Lord. What man is he that desireth life, And loveth many days, that he may see good? Keep thy tongue from evil, And thy lips from speaking guile. Depart from evil, and do good; Seek peace, and pursue it"—Psalm 34:11-14.

In the words of Psalm 34, children are invited to come and learn the secret of a happy life. The call appeals to the desire for happiness: "Who is he that would *see good?*" The teacher promises to show the path to the enjoyment of true well-being. That path is, "Depart from evil, and *do good.*" God has so ordered our nature that well-being will follow well-doing: to do good is the sure way to see good.

Our inspired teacher goes further. The Psalmist not only tells of our *seeing good* and *doing good*, but he teaches us the secret of *being good.* He tells us, "Come, ye children, hearken unto me; I will teach you the fear of the Lord." The fear of the Lord—this is the beginning of all wisdom and goodness. It is doing what we do, unto the Lord, for His sake and in obedience to Him. It is our personal relationship to God that makes conduct really good. To fear God—this is being good followed by doing good, then receiving good.

Christian parents have in this call, "Come, ye children, hearken unto Me," words prepared for them by the Holy Spirit to use with their children. They are God's ministers to teach the children the fear of the Lord, the path to the true, the highest good. Let us try and take these lessons to heart so that we can pass them on to our children.

Seeing Good

"What man is he that desireth life, and loveth many days, that he may *see good?*" Let parents not be afraid of promising their children that it shall be well with them if they do fear God. With the Creator of infinite goodness and wisdom, it cannot be otherwise. Doing right and pleasing Him must bring blessing and happiness. The desire for happiness should not be the only or the primary motive for a person's conduct. Experience has proved that those who make happiness their first objective fail. However, those who give it a second place to duty, find true happiness. God commands us to be happy. He promises us joy, but always in connection with our being in right relationship to Him and His will. The previous verse says, "They that seek the Lord shall not want any good thing" (Psalm 34:10).

There are many promises in God's Word that tell us He will do good for us. "I will surely do thee good" He said to Jacob (Genesis 32:12). To Israel He spake: "Do right and good, that it may be well with thee" (Deuteronomy 12:28). The principle expressed in the prayer, "Be good to them that do good," tells of the favor and friendship of God. His peace and presence, His guidance and help, will come to those who do His will. Obedience and doing good will bring blessings in this life, too. Let our children learn early that, if they will see good, it will be found with God. Let them learn it from us, not as a doctrine, but as a personal testimony. Let us show them that the service of God makes us happy, and that the good which God bestows is our one desire and our highest joy.

Doing Good

Let us seek in the hearts of our little ones to link well-doing with well-being. "Blessed is the man that feareth the Lord" (Psalm 112:1). The Christianity of our day has learned to seek safety in religion, but pleasure and happiness in the world. Our lives must provide clear evidence for our children that to *do God's will* and serve Him brings happiness and enjoyment. Nothing should be more important than teaching our children these lessons.

Let us study what doing good means. "Keep thy tongue from evil, and thy lips from speaking guile. Depart from evil, and do good; seek peace, and pursue it." Sins of the tongue, sins of disobedience, and sins of temper are the three principal temptations children are exposed to, and against which parents have to guard them.

Let the Christian parent strive for a deep conviction of the power of the tongue. The tongue reveals what is in the heart and sets it further on fire, by encouraging the speaking of the evil that is there. The tongue is the medium of speaking and influence on others. It indicates the presence or the lack of integrity which is the very foundation of true character. Parents, desire above everything to make your children true—first true in words, and then true in heart and deed. A child's honesty and integrity is the beginning of his walking in the truth of God. Let this be your goal, even with the little children: I have no greater joy than to hear that my children walk in the truth.

"Depart from evil, and do good." Anything a parent forbids is considered "evil" by a child. The parent is like a conscience. Train your little ones to flee from evil, to depart, to come away from everything naughty and forbidden. Keep him occupied, if possible, in what is good, doing those things which are allowed by you and pleasing to you. Strengthen his young will, train him to *do* good—not to think and wish and feel good, but to do it. It is what the will does that makes the person.

"Seek peace, and pursue it." Quarreling is a sin that comes so easily to children. Let us train them to respect the rights of others, to forgive when their rights are affected, and to seek justice only from the parent. "Blessed are the peacemakers, for they shall be called the children of God" (Matthew 5:9). This is one verse which children should be encouraged to practice.

Being Good

We must not only seek good, and do good, but *be good*. Only a good tree can bring forth good fruit. And what does it mean to be good? What kind of temperament makes the good man or the good child? "I will teach you the fear of the Lord." There is no one who is good but God. If we seek and find Him, we find all good. It is in the fear of the Lord that good behavior has its origin and virtue has its worth. "In singleness of heart, fearing God: and whatsoever ye do, do it heartily, as to the Lord" (Colossians 3:22,23). It is our personal relationship to God carried over into all our conduct that constitues the fear of the Lord. This kind of fear is closely related to hope and love. "The Lord taketh pleasure in them that *fear* Him, in those that hope in His mercy" (Psalm 147:11).

How can the fear of the Lord be taught? Dear Christian parents, you know the answer: only by yourselves walking in the fear of the Lord all day long. Seek to train your children to understand the connection between these three principles: *seeing good,* always being blessed and happy; *doing good,* a life in which we always choose what is right; and *being good,* having a heart filled with the fear and love of God. You can train them in these principles by living them yourself. Let them see you walk in the fear of the Lord. Let them recognize that His holy presence rests on you and is brought with you into daily life. Let them see in your conduct that Christianity is a power in the heart which moves the will in everything to do what is good. Let the light of your eyes and the brightness of your face be the evidence and the confirmation of God's truth, *"Blessed* is the man that feareth the Lord."

A Parent's Prayer

Lord God, I ask for grace to wisely apply the lessons of Your Word in dealing with my children. May my relationship with them be full of the joyful assurance that the fear of the Lord is the path to the enjoyment of all good. Help me to teach them that serving you is true happiness. Let this be so real that all thought of there being pleasure in the world may pass away. Help me to teach my children the fear of the Lord by instruction, example, and the spirit of my life. May thoughtfulness, truthfulness, and love characterize the climate of my home. May the lives of all those in my family be holy to the Lord. Day by day I desire to show them, through Your grace, how departing from every evil and doing good is what fearing the Lord teaches. Give me grace, above all, to teach them that the fear of the Lord itself is the true good, the principle of all good. Lord God, make me the parent You would have me to be, and let Your blessing rest on me and my home. Amen.

Chapter 21

FORMING HABITS IN YOUR CHILD

"Train up a child in the way he should go; and when he is old, he will not depart from it"—Proverbs 22:6.

This promise is the Scriptural expression of the principle on which all education rests: a child's training can decide what his life is to be. When this faith is elevated to a trust in God and His promises, it grows into the assurance that a parent's labor will not be in vain in the Lord. Everything will depend upon a correct view of what is "the way in which he should go." Only then can the training do its work in the assurance of the divine fulfillment of the promise.

There have been so many failures in religious training, that many parents doubt whether a principle like this can be regarded as holding true in all circumstances. With such doubt we undermine God's covenant. Instead, let us believe that the failure was man's fault. Either the parent did not make "the way in which he should go" his one aim in the child's training, or the training in that way was not what God's Word had ordered it to be. Let us see what the Word teaches us on each of these points.

The Way He Should Go

As to the way in which your child should go, we need have no doubts. God calls it, "the way of the Lord," when He speaks of Abraham training his children. We often read of "walking in His ways," "the way of His footsteps," "the way of His commandments." It is called "the way of wisdom," "the way of righteousness," "the way of holiness," "the way of peace," and "the way of life." It is "the new and living way" opened by Christ for all who will walk in His footsteps. It is Christ Himself, the living Way, of whom Scripture says, "Walk in Him."

There are many Christian parents who are anxious to see their children saved, but they do not choose this way for them. They do not decide on it distinctly as the one and only way in which they are to walk. They think it is too much to expect that their children should walk in it from their youth, and so they do not train them in that way. They are not prepared to regard the walking in this way as their primary objective. It is not their first aim to train whole-hearted devoted Christians. They will not give up their worldly interests. They are not always ready themselves to walk in that way only and completely—"the narrow way." They have chosen it, but not exclusively and finally. They have their own thoughts as to the way they and the child should go. No wonder that with a great deal of apparent religion the education of their children fails. Such a mistake is often fatal. There can be no doubt or hesitancy—"the way of the Lord" must be heartily accepted as the only "way in which he should go."

Train Up A Child

"In the way in which he should go, train up a child." *Train* is a word of deep importance for every teacher and parent to understand. It is not telling, not teaching, not commanding, but something higher than all these. Without training, teaching and commanding often do more harm than good. Training is not only telling a child what to do, but showing him how to do it and seeing that it is done. The parent must see to it that the advice or command given is put into practice and adopted as a habit.

What is needed for such training can be understood easily by looking at the way in which a young horse is trained. The young horse is made to yield its will to its master's, until at last it is in perfect harmony with him and yields to his slightest wish. How carefully the horse is directed and trained to do the right thing until it becomes a habit, a second nature! Its own wild nature, when necessary is checked and restrained. It is encouraged and helped to fully exercise its energies in subjection to its master's rule. Yet, everything is done to make it bold and spirited! The trainer is ready, at any difficulty, to help his horses. He will do anything to keep them from losing their confidence or being overcome by some difficulty they had to surmount! Watching this procedure I have often thought, "If only parents would take this kind of care in training their children in the way they should go!"

Training can now be defined in this way: getting the child accustomed to doing easily and willingly what the parent commands. Doing, doing habitually, doing from choice—this is what we aim for.

Doing Habitually

The parent who wishes to train not only tells or commands, but sees that the thing is done. Knowing how naturally careless and fickle a child's nature is, the parent encourages until the duty, which involves self-denial, is performed. The parent is careful not to give too many commands too hastily. He begins with commands which can be easily accomplished. By doing this, the child does not associate being obedient with the thought of what is displeasing or impossible. The parent can appeal to the motive of authority or of love, of duty or of pleasure. Most importantly, he must watch the child throughout the struggle. The parent must stay close by, until the consent of the child's will results in the deed being accomplished.

This is another element of training. Success in education depends more on forming habits than instilling rules. What the child has done once or twice he must learn to do over and over again, until it becomes familiar and natural. It must become so natural that it feels strange to him not to do it. Laziness and rebellion can come in and break the power of the growing habit. The parent silently watches. When there is danger of regression, he intervenes to help and confirm the habit until it is mastered. Going on from a first and a second command in which the child was obedient, the principle is extended until he feels it is natural for him to do the parent's will. In this way the habit of obedience is formed and becomes the root of other habits.

Doing From Choice

This is a higher objective because it is the true aim of education. You may have good, obedient children, who have seldom resisted your parental training. Yet, when left to themselves in later life, they depart from the way in which they were trained to go. The training was defective because the parents were content to teach habits without principles. The training of the young horse is not complete until he delights, full of joy and spirit, to do the work.

It is the training of the will that is the aim of education. Beginning with *obedience*, the parent has to lead the child on to *liberty* . These apparent opposites have to be reconciled in practice. To choose and will for himself what his parent wills, to find his happiness in obedience to the parent's command—this is what the child must be trained to do. This is the highest art, the real difficulty in training a child in the way he should go.

It is here the promise of divine grace becomes effective. No mind has yet understood the wonderful interaction of God's working and our working in the matter of the salvation of our children. However, we do not need to understand it to be sure of it. We can count on God's faithfulness. The believing parent seeks not only to form the habits of obedience, but by prayer and faith to guide and strengthen the will of the child in the way of the Lord. In doing this he can expect the workings of God's Holy Spirit to do what God alone can do. In covenant with God, the parent seeks to train his child's will. His will is made after the image of God's will, but now under the power of sin. The parent expects God's wisdom to guide him and he counts on divine strength to work with him and for him. He trusts in divine faithfulness to make this word true and sure in all its fullness, "Train up a child in the way he should go; when he is old, *he will not depart from it.*"

A Parent's Prayer

Lord, give me the spirit of wisdom, that I may understand the wonderful nature of my child's immortal spirit. Give me wisdom, that I may know the way in which the child should go, even the way of Your footsteps. Let me so walk in Your way that he may learn from me that, there is no other way pleasing to You, and there is no other way that can give us true pleasure. Give me wisdom, that I may know how to guide and influence my child's will, so that he may give himself first to my will, and then to Yours to choose only and always Your way. Lord, give me wisdom to train my child in the way he should go, even the way of the Lord. Amen.

Chapter 22

THE CHILD'S WILL AND CONSCIENCE

"He may know to refuse the evil, and choose the good"—Isaiah 7:15.

Of all the wonderful powers with which God has endowed man, his will—the power of determining what he does, and so what he is—is the most wonderful. This is the deepest trait of the divine image. Just as God was of Himself and not of another, so He gave man to a very large extent the power of deciding and making himself. The mind of man, the soul with all its emotions, man's moral and religious nature—all these have been given for man to make decisions and fashion his own being and destiny for eternity.

The parent has been entrusted with the solemn task of teaching the child how to use his will in the right way. This delicate instrument is put into the hands of the parents to keep, to direct, and to strengthen. The parent must train the child to exercise his will for the glory of the God who gave it. To those who seek wisdom from God to fulfill their task, success is possible and promised.

Developing Obedience

To combine the greatest degree of personal liberty with perfect obedience is a very delicate problem. God's Word has more than once taught that obedience is the child's first virtue. He is to obey, not because he understands or approves, but because the parent commands. In this he is to become the master of his own will by voluntarily submitting it to a higher authority. Obedience from this principle will secure a double blessing for the child. While guiding the will to form right habits, it strengthens the control the child has over his will. When this has been attained, a sure foundation has been laid for the exercise of the child's free will choosing what appears to him to be best.

In the first stage of childhood, *before the child knows* to refuse evil and choose good, simple obedience is law. It is this that the parent must regard as his highest and most blessed work. As the child matures, it is still a parent's influence that must train the young will to exercise the power on which everything in his later life depends. The child must now be trained himself to refuse evil and choose good.

Training The Child's Will

How is this to be done? The decisions of the will depend upon the impulses and motives which prompt it to action. These impulses and motives again depend upon the objects presented to the mind, and the degree of attention they are given. In our fallen nature, the soul is stimulated far more by the visible and the temporal, than by the unseen and the real. The soul is deceived by what appears pleasing or beautiful. The influence of what is present outweighs that of the future, even though it may be of infinitely greater worth.

It is the work of the parent to present to the child the best reasons for taking certain actions and help him to refuse evil and choose good. The parent must present to the child the beauty of virtue, the nobility and happiness of self-denial, the pleasure that duty brings, and the fear and the favor of God. The parent creates positive emotions within the child which cause him to gladly will to choose to do good.

Training The Child's Conscience

The parent acts as a conscience for the child, calling him to be true to his higher instincts and convictions. The parent leads him to the true pleasure with which duty rewards even the young. The training of the child aims especially at teaching him to refuse evil and choose good when there is no parent nearby to help. The conscience of every person is a guardian and helper of inestimable value in choosing the path of right. Wise training can do much to establish the authority of this inner rule. Proper training will lead the child to look upon his conscience; not as a spy, but as his truest friend and best companion.

The authority of the parent and of conscience

should be linked together, so that even in the parent's absence, the weight of his influence may be felt. The success of all true education involves helping the pupil to teach himself. Therefore, the aim and success of moral training must be to form in the child the habit of ruling himself and always listening to the inward monitor. Cultivate in the child the mental skills of reflection and quiet meditation, so that he may always wait to listen for the gentle inner whisper that tells him to refuse evil and choose good.

The Final Authority

Conscience, however, can only tell to do the right but it cannot always teach what the right is. The mind may be wrong in its views of good and evil, and faithfulness to conscience may even lead the child to choose evil and refuse good. The inner light shines upon the path of what we think is duty. It is only the light from above that shows what that duty really is. "Thy Word is a lamp unto my feet, and a light unto my path" (Psalm 119:105).

One of the most precious influences of a godly education is the consent of the heart to take God's Word as the standard of good and evil, and the desire to let it decide in every choice. The authority of the parent, of conscience, of God's Word is a threefold cord that cannot be broken. This cord binds the child to the throne and the will of God, where he knows to refuse evil and choose good.

We need hardly repeat again how such training

141

is not to take the place of divine grace, but to be its servant. It prepares the way for God's Spirit by forming a strong and intelligent will to be later used in God's service. It follows up the work of grace by guiding it in the path where all God's perfect will is to be accepted as the rule of conduct. The kind of training that teaches the child to refuse evil and choose good is of unspeakable value.

When the parent realizes the meaning of the words good and evil, he will see how in every step of life there are two motives struggling to be master. Choosing between evil and good is a lifelong task which is carried out every day. The parent will recognize the great responsibility entrusted to him of awakening, guiding, and strengthening the young will of his child. The parent will feel that if he can do this one thing well, he has done his highest work. To know to refuse evil and choose good will be to choose Christ and holiness and eternal life.

Dear parents, God's highest gift to man was the freedom to *choose* the will of his God. Your highest work is to take charge of that will in your child and be God's minister in helping your child choose His service. Realize your own incompetency to influence your child's will in which the powers of light and darkness are wrestling for supremacy. Depend upon the leading of the Holy Spirit for the renewal of your child. May it be your reward and his joy to see his will given up to choose good, to choose God.

A Parent's Prayer

Lord God, teach me to form and train the will of my child to refuse evil and choose good. Make me very gentle and patient with a sense of my own willfulness. Make me faithful to fulfill my duties as a parent, trusting in You because You are my help and my Father. Amen.

Chapter 23

GOD'S SPIRIT IN YOUR CHILD

"I will pour my Spirit upon thy seed, and my blessing upon thine offspring. . .One shall say, I am the Lord's. . .and another shall subscribe with his hand unto the Lord"—Isaiah 44:3,5.

In the prophecy of the outpouring of the Holy Spirit, quoted by Joel on the day of Pentecost, mention is made of the sons and daughters. In Isaiah the blessing of an outpoured Spirit is also made to the seed and offspring of God's people. The root-principle of the covenant, promising grace to the fathers for the children, to the children for the fathers' sake and through the fathers, is to be the mark of the outpouring of the Spirit, too. This promise is accompanied by the very distinct statement of what would be the fruit of the Spirit's coming on the offspring. Not content with a religion inherited from their fathers, the children openly profess their personal faith in the words: "I am the Lord's." The child's personal acknowledgment of the Lord is the fruit of the Spirit's work.

The Child's Profession Of Faith

All Christian parents desire that, as their children grow up, they will make personal confession of the faith in which they have been raised. If we enter fully into the mind of God, it will be one of our great aims to raise our children to make such a profession.

However, there are many Christian parents who would hesitate to admit this. To some the dangers of giving their children a distinctly religious education appears so great that they leave their children to themselves. They would never think of asking them if they can say, I am the Lord's, or encouraging them to do so. They do not believe in the conversion of children. They think that children are so impressionable, that such a profession is not to be taken seriously and ought to be avoided.

Other parents are themselves in the dark on what they consider to be the intricate question of assurance of faith. Because they themselves have no liberty to say, I am the Lord's, it is no wonder they never think of encouraging their children to say it. They think it is only the advanced believer who dares make such a profession. For them it would be considered as presumption and pride to say they are the Lord's.

Other parents admit in theory the duty of making such a confession. Their hearts are so cold and worldly that the warm, loving confession of Jesus as their Lord is never heard from their lips. Family worship and religious profession testify to anything but the living, loving attachment to a personal Savior. Their children would never learn from them to say, I am the Lord's.

In Isaiah 44:3,5 it is distinctly promised that the Spirit will manifest Himself in a living spiritual faith. Experience has proved to many that a distinct profession of Jesus as Savior is as sure a fruit of the Spirit's presence among children as among older people. This experience of salvation can be just as reliable for children as for adults.

A little reflection will convince us that nothing can be more natural than this fruit of God's blessing on the labors of believing parents. Do we not tell them from their youth that God is love and that He gave Jesus to be our Savior? Do we not tell them that they belong to God, not only by right of creation and redemption, but by virtue of His having accepted them? Why, then, should it appear strange if the child believes what we say and speaks out, I am the Lord's? We tell them that Jesus receives sinners who confess their sins and give themselves to Him to be cleansed. This truly is what we ought to hope for as the fruit of our instruction. When the child is aware of his sins, he goes and confesses them to the blessed children's Friend. He believes that Jesus does not reject him, but accepts and pardons.

Let us be very careful of casting suspicion on the childlike profession, I am the Lord's! We teach the children that this statement implies a giving of ourselves to be God's property, to do His will, and to acknowledge Him as Lord and Master. If their young hearts are touched, we must not doubt their profession or reproach them when they fail. Let us remember the promised fruit of the Spirit's working among the children is this: I am the Lord's.

The Promise Of The Spirit

We have been warning against doubting the reality of a child's conversion and profession of faith. God's Word teaches us that the Holy Spirit will make the child's experience of salvation real and sincere. Let us consider the second lesson the prophecy from Isaiah teaches: it is the Spirit's working that will make the "I am the Lord's" become reality for the child.

In what way is the outpouring of the Spirit to be given? The promise was fulfilled on the day of Pentecost! The Spirit dwells in the Church of Christ, in the hearts and the homes of His believing disciples. There may come special outpourings of the Spirit in revival movements when the young come forward in numbers to confess their Lord. However, we do not have to wait for revival. In promising the Spirit to the offspring of His people, God wants us to expect that parental instruction and a consecrated home life are used by the Spirit to lead the children to Christ. The Spirit always works in the Word and the parent is the God-ordained minister of the Word. The blessing of the promise is that the parent may claim the Holy Spirit for his children. All the parent's teaching and training are a demonstration of the Spirit and of power.

Everything depends upon the parent himself as a minister of the Spirit. He must live and walk, he must be led and sanctified by the Spirit. He must speak and pray in the Spirit. He must in faith claim and accept the promise of the Spirit for his child. A child's profession depends greatly on the parent's profession. If theirs is a language of joyous faith, the child catches the meaning from the spirit in which he sees these words lived out. If the parents continually speak words of encouragement, even when the child fails, he will see the reality of the change which their profession has brought about.

Dear parents, let God's thoughts for your children enter your hearts and rule there. Remember these thoughts. God's Spirit and my children belong to each other. I may in faith claim the Spirit's dwelling and working in them. The fruit of the Spirit is the faith that causes my child to confess, Jesus is mine. Let this promise be your strength as you deal with God and with your child: They that wait on the Lord shall not be ashamed.

A Parent's Prayer

Lord God, we draw near to You to claim the fulfillment of this promise on behalf of our beloved children. Lord, may they from their very youth have Your Spirit poured out upon them, that even in the simplicity of childhood they may say, I am the Lord's. Please fill us with Your Holy Spirit. May our home life and our parental influence be a channel through which the Spirit reaches each child. Help us to live in such a way that the life surrounding our children may be life in the Spirit. Gracious Lord, make it our one aim to train our children for You alone. Teach us to understand that the indwelling of the blessed Spirit is not something hardly to be expected, but the one gift the Father loves to bestow. Help us to realize that the Holy Spirit is the first gift a child needs to grow as a believing Christian. May we experience the wonderful blending of the parent's work and the Spirit's work in securing the seed of Your people for Yourself. Amen.

Chapter 24

FROM GENERATION TO GENERATION

"My righteousness shall be for ever, and my salvation from generation to generation"—Isaiah 51:8.

When we speak of a generation in the history of man, we think of the shortness of human life and the continual change among men. "One generation passeth away, and another generation cometh: but the earth abideth for ever" (Ecclesiastes 1:4). What a contrast between man and the heavens and mountains around him—always the same. What a contrast between man, whose life is but a span, and the unchangeable, everlasting God.

The Two Sides

We shall find that God's Word loves not so much to contrast as to link together these opposites. The Bible lifts man out of the transience of life, to find his refuge in the unchangeableness of God. "As for man, his days are as grass. . .but the mercy of the Lord is from everlasting to everlasting upon them that fear Him, and His righteousness unto children's children" (Psalm 103:15,17). "O my God, take me not away in the midst of my days: Thy years are throughout all generations. . .(The earth and the heavens) shall perish, but *Thou shalt endure*. . .but Thou art the same, and Thy years shall have no end. The children of Thy servants *shall continue* and their seed shall be established before Thee" (Psalm 102:24,26-28). Death may separate one generation from another, but God's mercy connects them, passing on from one to another. His everlasting righteousness reveals itself as salvation from generation to generation.

At every point where God meets and acts with man, there are two sides to be regarded—the divine and the human. This is also true in the transmission of God's salvation from generation to generation. God's faithfulness inspires salvation in man, and therefore demands and rewards it. In some passages it might almost appear as if everything depends upon man and his keeping the covenant; it does, indeed. It is not as if this keeping of the covenant were to be man's work, by which he secures the blessing. Instead, it is in the mercy and truth of God that human faithfulness has its strength and security. To know God's purpose and to believe God's promise communicates to the soul the very spirit of His faithfulness. This binds us firmly to Him; He, who is "all in all," can work out His purpose in us.

The Divine Side Of Salvation

Let us look at the divine side of this salvation

from generation to generation. In Isaiah this truth is expressed with great frequency: "As for Me, this is My covenant with them, saith the Lord; My Spirit that is upon thee, and My words which I have put in thy mouth, shall not depart out of thy mouth, nor out of the mouth of thy seed, nor out of the mouth of thy seed's seed, from henceforth and for ever" (Isaiah 59:21). This passage refers to New Testament times.

When God made His covenant with David, He anticipated generations in which there would be disobedience, and therefore punishment. (See 2 Samuel 7:14 and Psalm 89:30-33.) The promise of the Spirit and the Word in the mouth of God's Anointed One and His people is not to depart from the mouth of the seed's seed. There are families in which generations, and even centuries, the Word and the Spirit have not departed from the mouth of their children or their children's children. Let us only open our hearts to take in the promise, and to let it grow within us.

Then, we have that other beautiful promise: "I will direct their work in truth, and I will make an everlasting covenant with them. And their seed shall be known among the Gentiles, and their off-spring among the people: all that see them shall acknowledge them, that they are the seed which the Lord hath blessed" (Isaiah 61:8,9). Or, as it is otherwise expressed: "They are the seed of the blessed of the Lord, and their offspring with them" (Isaiah 65:23). The covenant with Abraham and David was also an everlasting covenant, but its fulfillment was accomplished in spite of the generations that proved faithless.

However, in the power of the promised Spirit, believing parents may claim and expect from child to child, to see the blessing of the Lord. This is to be the fruit of the outpouring of the Holy Spirit. The promise, "Thou, and thy son, and thy son's son" (Deuteronomy 6:2) is to have its literal fulfillment. This is not only for our comfort and joy, and the blessing on our children, but that God may be known and glorified. "Their seed shall be known among the Gentiles" (Isaiah 61:9). They are to be God's witnesses on earth, if need be, among the Gentiles to the end of the earth. For this reason, the Word and the Spirit are not to depart from the mouth of our seed from henceforth and for evermore.

The Human Side Of Salvation

Let us look now at the human side of the fulfillment of this promise: "My salvation from generation to generation." Most strikingly God's purpose is set forth in these words: "We will not hide them from their children, shewing to the generation to come the praises of the Lord, and His strength, and His wonderful works that He hath done" (Psalm 78:4). Then we read: "One generation shall praise Thy works to another" (Psalm 145:4). The triumphant joy of that psalm of praise reflects the spirit in which parents should tell their child of God's glory and goodness.

Here we have the human side. Parents who

153

know God show His praise, His strength, and His wonderful works to their children. Parental instruction is in the ministry of the Spirit, testifying for God in the spirit of praise, telling what He has done for us. The children are taught not to forget the works of God, but to set their hope on Him and keep His commandments, to trust and to obey Him. In this way, His righteousness, which is from everlasting to everlasting, becomes salvation from generation to generation.

Parents, it is God's will that His salvation should be from generation to generation in your family, too. Your children should hear from you and pass on to their children the praise of the Lord. Let us seek to enter into God's plans, and with our whole heart labor earnestly to secure the blessing and to please our Father! We know what is needed—nothing but wholehearted devotion to God. Nothing less will do. God's salvation must not be a secondary thing that is to be enjoyed along with the things of the world. The salvation of our children must be our first priority. We must set our whole heart upon it, even as God does.

This must be the one thing we live for—to glorify God. Such a life will prove to our children the joy of God's salvation and will influence them to also be saved. It is this whole-hearted devotion that will give strength to our faith and confidence to our hope. Under its inspiration our prayers will be persevering and believing. It will impart to our instruction the joyful tone of assurance, and make our whole life the model for our children. It is one generation living for God that will secure the next for Him. I must expect that my whole-hearted consecration to God will guide them, because His salvation is from generation to generation.

A Parent's Prayer

Lord God, let Your word, "my salvation from generation to generation," fill my heart. Make my calling and duty, along with Your promise and purpose, equally clear to me. Then I will know that the salvation of my children is as sure as my own. Lord, grant that in Your light I may realize and manifest fully what salvation is—salvation from sin and its power unto the holiness and the service of God. Lord God, give me grace to make salvation the one heirloom my children cherish. May the one thing transmitted in our home from child to child, be the salvation, the love, the joy, the service of God. Yes, Lord, You are the Eternal and Unchanging One—let it be so from generation to generation. Amen.

Chapter 25

YOUR CHILD—GOD'S PROPHET

"I will pour out my Spirit upon all flesh; and your sons and your daughters shall prophesy"—Joel 2:28.

This promise was fulfilled on the day of Pentecost. Christ promised the coming of the Comforter, the baptism with the Holy Spirit and with fire, to His disciples to make them His witnesses to the end of the earth. All these precious promises of Christ were comprehended and fulfilled in Joel's prophecy. The Holy Spirit is the Church's power for testimony and for suffering, for triumph and for blessing. The Spirit is the heavenly sign with which the Church has been marked and sealed.

In this prophetic promise, the children are given an important place: "Your *sons and daughters* shall prophesy, your old men shall dream dreams, your *young men* shall see visions" (Joel 2:28). The seed of God's people have such a place in His heart that, when He deals with His people, their offspring are continually in His thoughts.

Even in this promise of Pentecost, the first thing introduced is not that the disciples are now anointed to preach, but the sons and the daughters are prepared to prophesy. Just try and understand what this teaches us about God's purpose, a parent's hope, and a child's education.

God's Purpose

With the gift of the Holy Spirit to His Church, God's objective was to give power from on high to do the work of testifying to the ends of the earth. (See Acts 1:8.) All the other blessings of the Spirit: assurance, joy, holiness, and love have this as their aim—influence, fruit-bearing, the power to bless. If there were a wholehearted surrender to God's service and work, the blessing of the Spirit would come easily. No wise man wastes power: he economizes it, and uses just what is necessary for the work. We receive the power of the Spirit according to our faith.

This is true of our children, too. In Joel's prophecy God reveals His purpose with our sons and daughters. Under the mighty breathings of His Spirit they are to prophesy. Paul tells us what this prophesying means: "If all *prophesy*, and there come in one that believeth not, or one unlearned, he is convinced of all, he is judged of all: and thus are the secrets of his heart made manifest; and so falling down on his face he will worship God, and report that God is in you of a truth" (1 Corinthians 14:24,25). This is prophesying in the power of the Spirit, convicting even the unbelieving and

157

unlearned. *God wants our sons and daughters to be this kind of prophet.* We ought to educate our sons and daughters in such a way that they can become the prophet God wants.

The Church is suffering for lack of such prophets. Supply always creates demand. Because there is a small supply of such prophets, the Church thinks it has done something great when there is annually some increase in the number of its pastors and evangelists. If the Church and parents understood what glory it is to train our sons and daughters to be prophets of the Most High, witnesses and messengers for Jesus our Lord, what a change it would bring in our methods of operation!

The children of this world strive to obtain some high commission in the army or navy, or some good appointment in the civil service or in business. The children of God should press around the throne of their Father, seeking that He would fulfill this promise in their children and make them His prophets wherever He has need of them. God's purpose is that the Holy Spirit should take possession of our sons and daughters for His service. They belong to Him, and He to them.

The Parent's Hope

If parents were to train their children for the service of God's Spirit, they would no longer need to doubt whether their children would be saved. Aim high and you will accomplish more than the parent who is content with a lower goal. Consecration aims at the highest that God has promised. The secondary gifts, that others struggle for in vain, are given to them as well. Nothing will give such confidence of the salvation of our children as the knowledge of having surrendered our children undividedly to the service of God and His Spirit.

This surrender will equally inspire us with confidence in regard to our fitness for parental duty. We have no conception of the extent to which self-interest weakens faith and self-sacrifice strengthens it. If I know I am seeking the salvation of my children for their own and for my sake, I will not be able to believe that God will give me grace for training my child. But, if I lose all selfish thought of myself and my children and place them at God's disposal, then I am sure that my Father will give me grace for the work I do for Him.

Although I may not see each child used in the direct service of the Master, I can be sure that my training has influenced them, whatever their calling in life may be. The more distinct my acknowledgment that the Spirit claims all, the more I can depend upon His presence with me and mine.

The Children's Training

Cultivate the child's every mental ability with the purpose of having a sharp instrument prepared for the Master's use. Cultivate their natural virtues such as, diligence and decision, order and method, promptness and firmness. Cultivate these with the high aim of having the child better equipped for the work to be done. Make these your highest goals in training your child for Christ: obedience to conscience and to law, self-control and temperance, strict integrity and justice, humility and love. Then the Holy Spirit can form the child into a sincere Christian, an efficient servant of the Lord, a true prophet.

There have been those parents who willingly suffered need in order to give their sons a good education or to secure their daughters a high position in society. Let us set our hearts upon the spiritual promotion we seek for our children, with no thought of sacrifices. We must study and labor to pray and believe, so that our children will be counted worthy of a place among the separated ones whom the Spirit of the Lord anoints for His work.

Now we close our meditations on the Old Testament evidence as to the place children occupy in the purpose and promise of God. We have seen *what God wants to be for our children*—a God in covenant, with the covenant blessing of the blood and the Spirit of Jesus. We have seen *what He would have our children be to Him*—a covenant seed, to receive and transmit and multiply the blessing throughout the earth. We have seen *what He would have parents be* —the ministers of the covenant, to sprinkle and plead the blood with Him for their children. Parents are to receive the Spirit from Him, and by example and training and life to communicate the blessing to their children. Parents are to be the channels for the Spirit's training of their children for His service.

160

May God help us to learn these three lessons. May God help us to believe and receive all He is willing to be for our children through us. May God help us to give and train the children for all He would have them be. May God help us to be faithful to seek for our children nothing less than God seeks. May we, as parents, live in such a way that, from our homes, sons and daughters may go forth to prophesy in His name.

A Parent's Prayer

Lord, fulfill Your promise to our children. Give us grace to train them for You in the faith of the Spirit's working. Give us grace to prepare them to be equipped for the Master's use, every gift cultivated and consecrated for Your service. Let our sons and daughters prophesy in the power of the Holy Spirit. Lord, bless all believing parents who recognize Your claim on their children and know the high privilege of offering their children to You for service. We yield our children to You to be used as prophets of the Most High. May all their training be in harmony with Your purpose: "Your sons and daughters shall prophesy." Amen.

Chapter 26

THE HEAVENLY AND THE EARTHLY FATHER

"If ye then, being evil, know how to give good gifts unto your children, how much more shall your Father which is in heaven give good gifts to them that ask Him?"—Matthew 7:11.

We began our meditations on the Old Testament with man created in the image of God, and the home on earth as a picture of the home in heaven. The New Testament gives a fuller revelation of the Father in heaven. We will begin our New Testament lessons studying what God means family life to be, and what we are to be to our children.

The Role Of The Father On Earth

Jesus wants us to learn from our experiences of being a father on earth to know the Father in heaven. God is the true Father. His very nature is the God of Love. Fatherhood was the glory and the blessedness of the divine being. Our fatherhood on earth has been given as a reflection of His, and to lead us to a participation in its honor and joy. We, too, are to taste the blessedness of producing a child in our likeness. In him, we will find the object of our love, the reflection of our image, and a companion and helper in all our work.

Because this fatherhood in heaven is beyond our comprehension, we must study the father-heart on earth to get a more complete understanding of what God is to us. The deepest mysteries of God's love are best studied by a parent in his own heart and emotions. We think of our love to our children, the joy they give us, the sympathy their troubles awaken, and the patient kindness their waywardness requires. Jesus wants us to look at God the Father and consider *how much more* all this must be in God the Good and Perfect One, than in us who are evil. He wants us to banish every shadow of unbelief from the heart, and live our life in the sunshine of God's love.

A parent can exert tremendous influence on his child. He is able to breath his own thoughts and ideas, and even his own will into his child. In the same way the Father in heaven loves us and is able to breathe His own mind, His own Spirit, into us. As parents, we strive to secure the love and obedience of our children, longing for them to find their happiness in our will, our friendship, and our company. In the same way, the Father loves to meet us in secret and hear us speak to Him. The loving trust of His child brings the Father in heaven great joy. What a study for every father and mother to see their child respond to them and return their love. So, in the light of the fatherhood on earth, we can better understand the fatherhood in heaven.

The Example Of The Heavenly Father

The fatherhood in heaven will also cast its light on the fatherhood of earth, and teach us what we ought to be. By giving us the place, the name, and the power of *father,* God has in a very real sense made us His image-bearers. He expects us to do our work as parents, to copy Him, to act like Him as much as possible. Parents who desire to bring a full blessing to their children must make God's fatherhood their model and their example. They must enter into God's purpose, make it their own, and pursue it with their whole heart. From Him, parents will learn to combine love with authority, and bring about their child's hearty surrender to all God's will. In the tenderness, patience and self-sacrifice of the divine love, in the firmness and righteousness of divine rule, the parent will find the secret of successful training.

From the Father, we can learn how very personal such training is. The Father has come down to us in Christ. By His own example, He shows us that He wants us to be as He is. By giving us His Spirit, He teaches us that fatherhood longs to draw the child into perfect likeness and oneness with Himself. The earthly father will come to understand that the highest duty of our fatherhood *is just to be what the child is to be*. A father must breathe his own spirit into the child. As a child of the heavenly Father, the parent receives His Spirit day by day. He also breathes this into his child.

Being a parent is a serious, but most blessed, occupation. The parent is the image of the heavenly Father, His picture to the child on earth.

The Reflection Of The Heavenly Father

The earthly father must see the Father in heaven as his model and guide. The parent must reflect God so that the child will naturally look from him, whom he sees, to the unseen One whom he represents. A child loves his parents by natural instinct. As the child sees in the father all that is holy and worthy of honor, this natural love becomes devotion and reverence. In a Christian father, a child ought to have a better example than the best sermon can give. The father should reflect the love and care of the heavenly Father with blessing and joy. To attain this, the parent must distinctly aim at making himself the ladder by which the child can climb to the Father above. The child must see in his parents the joy that Christianity brings. Then, the name of God as Father will become linked with all that is lovely and holy in the memory of a child. In this way the fatherhood on earth will be the gate to the Father's home above.

Is it possible to live in such a way that all this could be true? The one thing the Father loves to give, is His own Holy Spirit—His Father-Spirit to be in us the spirit of a son. We have only to believe, receive, and yield to the Spirit. He will make our fatherhood the image of God's, and from us there will flow streams of living water to bless our children.

What a world it would be if every Christian father was determined to realize and fulfill his calling. How wonderful it would be if in a holy partnership with the Father in heaven, he yielded himself to be taught, sanctified, and used to train children for the Father who is in heaven.

A Parent's Prayer

Our Father in heaven, give us more insight into Your Fatherhood. Help us to see how You command and expect that our fatherhood should be the reflection of Your own. May they indeed be one; one in purpose, one in method, one in principle, one in spirit. O God, we want to be fathers to our children, just as You are to us. Make us such, so that You can fully use us as the channels for Your grace to our little ones. May they see in us true pictures of Him to whom we teach them to say, Our Father which art in heaven. Father, we look to Your Son for the answer to our prayer. We count upon the tenderness and the faithfulness of Your love and Your mighty power and Spirit to bless the parents of Your Church who pray to You. Amen.

Chapter 27

CHILDREN OF THE KINGDOM

"But the children of the kingdom shall be cast out into outer darkness"—Matthew 8:12.

What close union we have here before us in the wonderful privilege and the terrible danger that our children have in the Church of Christ. They are children of the Kingdom: how glorious! They can be cast out into outer darkness: how awful! The only way to avoid the latter is to fully grasp the former. To this end let us try to understand all this implies.

Children of the Kingdom! What Kingdom? The answer is simple: the Kingdom of God! *Where is this Kingdom?* In heaven—it is that divine dominion which rules in heaven and the whole heavenly world. Its center is the Throne of God, where the Holy One dwells, and from whom all life and all law and all love flow forth. Around that Throne are powers and principalities and dominions, with their untold myriads of angels who do His will and are the messengers of His power. In God's Kingdom everything is love and blessing; in His subjects everything is obedience and joy.

How can this heavenly Kingdom be here on earth? When God created the heavens and the earth, it was to secure new territory in which His heavenly empire might be established. But the power of another kingdom, the kingdom of Satan, interfered. The coming of the Kingdom was delayed in the fall of man. For four thousand years it was promised and hoped for, but the Kingdom of heaven was not yet on earth.

How did this Kingdom come? In the fullness of time, the King Himself came to earth. The message was given: The Kingdom of heaven is at hand, the Kingdom of heaven is come unto you. The King came, first in His own life as a subject and a servant. Jesus came to show us the spirit that indwells all the subjects of the Kingdom—implicit obedience, and a delight in doing the will of God. In that obedience unto death, Jesus broke the power of Satan and of sin. He showed forth the wondrous love and set us free for a life of obedience like His own. Then, as King, He ascended to heaven and took His seat upon the throne. It was then the Kingdom could come. In the outpouring of the Holy Spirit, the Kingdom came in power. It was set up in the hearts of those who had been prepared to receive Him and to enter the Kingdom.

Who were the subjects of this Kingdom? Jesus said: "Except a man be born again, he cannot see the kingdom of God" (John 3:3). Nothing less than the Spirit of God coming in and taking possession of a person can equip him to enter. Only the Spirit of heaven could make it possible for a person to see the Kingdom or live as one of its subjects. Jesus also said: "Blessed are the poor in spirit: for theirs is the kingdom of heaven" (Matthew 5:3). To become an heir of the Kingdom, nothing was needed except the confession of spiritual poverty; so that having nothing, we might possess all.

What are the characteristics of those who truly belong to this Kingdom? They are the characteristics by which the King was known on earth: love towards God, obedience to the uttermost, and an absolute surrender to His will. He had love for all people, gave himself to live and die, and brought the blessings of the Kingdom to all who would believe. "The kingdom of God is not in word but in power" (1 Corinthians 4:20). The Kingdom of heaven is in the infinite power of the eternal life. As the Kingdom comes down, the Holy Spirit, the power, also comes to give the strength to live as members of the Kingdom. In each person of the Kingdom, the prayer, "Thy kingdom come," becomes the desire of the heart. Everything else in life becomes secondary to the Kingdom's extension and the manifestation of its glory.

Who are the children of the Kingdom? Jesus spoke this word even of the Jews who rejected the Kingdom. God had in His great mercy committed the promise of the Kingdom to Israel, and all its children were its heirs. Now, our children are born under the Kingdom's influence and destined for its blessings. Our children are children of the

Kingdom—"of such is the kingdom of heaven."

What is needed to secure for our children the possession of the Kingdom to which they have been made the heirs? It is possible for them to lose it—"children of the kingdom may be cast out into outer darkness." They must be educated and trained under the influence and power of the heavenly life, in the very spirit of the Kingdom. In this way the blessing of the Kingdom may become their own personal and everlasting possession.

Who is to train our children? Christian parents, this is our holy privilege! As children of the Kingdom, they are entrusted to us to keep and nourish. The keynote of our teaching, the watchword in all our efforts on their behalf, must be this: They are children of the Kingdom. To parents God has entrusted the high commission of leading their children on to the life of possession and full enjoyment of the Kingdom.

What is needed to enable the parent to do this? The parent himself must live in and for the Kingdom of heaven. The atmosphere of the home must be the spirit of heaven. Christ's command, "Seek ye first the kingdom of God" (Matthew 6:33) must be the ruling principle of all conduct in the home. The child must receive the impression that not only personal blessing, but the interests and extension of God's Kingdom are the hope and the joy of life. Parents whose citizenship is in heaven, who have in truth entered the Kingdom and live in it, will alone be found worthy to train their children as heirs of the Kingdom.

How can parents live for the Kingdom? "My kingdom," Jesus said, "is not of this world. . .My kingdom is not from hence" (John 18:36). It is from above, from heaven, from God, that the Kingdom comes daily. Coming out of the world, we can daily enter into the Holy Place within the veil through the blood. The believer must *spend time in God's presence* in worship and surrender, until the anointing is fresh upon him. Only in this way can the Spirit come down into his home and consecrate it for the children of the Kingdom.

As long as we are content with just enough religion to save ourselves and our children, we must not be surprised if they remain unsaved. It is only as we *seek to be filled with the Spirit* and to have our whole life sacrificed for the Kingdom, that we may count on the blessing of successful spiritual training for our children. Jesus said, "My kingdom is not of this world." The spirit of the world ruling in the parents destroys all that they hope to accomplish by their purposes, their teaching, or their prayers. In Christ's command, "First the kingdom," we have the secret and the certainty of successful spiritual training for our children.

Parents, your children are children of the Kingdom, the Kingdom of God in heaven! Hold and love and train them for God alone. From God alone is your hope and your help. Seek it in much prayer. Accept it in childlike faith, believing that you will receive what you ask. *Yield yourself to God,* denying self, not allowing self any say in the guidance of your life or home. Yield yourself to

God, keeping an ear open every hour to hear the voice of the Holy Spirit, who alone can work in us the laws and the powers of the Kingdom.

Above all, remember Jesus! He said, "Suffer the little children to come unto Me. . .for of such is the kingdom of God" (Mark 10:14). He is the King: in Him we have the Kingdom as a Presence. *Live with Jesus,* in Him. He loves our children and looks after them. His presence and love will more than anything fill us and them with a holy enthusiasm for the Kingdom. They will grow up in the Kingdom and for the Kingdom. We shall taste the unspeakable joy of having our home within the Kingdom and having the Kingdom of heaven within our home.

A Parent's Prayer

Father, we look to Your Father-love to give us, who are fathers and mothers, grace to realize how sacred is our calling and our home, because we are training children of the Kingdom for You. Blessed Lord Jesus, who said of the little ones, "Of such is the kingdom," we ask You to reveal to us Your Kingdom in its spiritual reality and glory. Reveal to us Your Kingdom here on earth as the rule of God by the Holy Spirit in the hearts and lives of His people. May the Kingdom of God be within us in such power so that the very atmosphere in our home will really make them children of the Kingdom. Amen.

Chapter 28

A MOTHER'S PERSEVERING PRAYER

"A woman of Canaan came. . .and cried unto Him, saying, Have mercy on me, O Lord, thou Son of David; my daughter is grievously vexed with a devil. . . .Then Jesus answered and said unto her, O woman, great is thy faith: be it unto thee even as thou wilt"—Matthew 15:22,28.

In the Old Testament we found God's promises of blessing on the godly training of children very clear and sure. His warnings on the neglect of this duty were also very distinct. In more than one tragic example we saw with what relentless power the warning came true. In the sons of Aaron and Eli, in the family of David and Solomon, proof was given that the personal righteousness of the father could not save the ungodly child. We found no answer to one of the most solemn questions that can be asked, and which has burned in many a parent's heart: Is there still hope for a sinful child who is going out beyond the reach of a parent's influence?

The Wandering Child

In Christ Jesus, God has revealed how completely the power of sin and Satan has been broken. It is in Christ Jesus that God has shown us what it is possible for His grace to do. It is in Christ Jesus, too, we must seek for the answer to every question of a parent's heart. In His earthly life it is revealed to us all that Jesus and the Father are willing to do for us. We find what His mighty saving power will do for a wandering child.

As we study this carefully, we will be surprised to find that the most precious and encouraging words of Christ were spoken to parents regarding their children. "Be not afraid, only believe" (Mark 5:36). "All things are possible to him that believeth" (Mark 9:23). "O woman, great is thy faith: be it unto thee even as thou wilt" (Matthew 15:28). These words are the parents' property. They give the blessed assurance that there is no case in which a child, now in Satan's power, is beyond the reach of a Savior's love and a parent's faith.

Let us see how wonderfully this will come out in the well-known story of the Syrophenician mother. Let us think of her daughter's misery, her prayer's refusal, her faith's perseverance, and her rich reward.

Her Daughter's Misery

"My daughter is grievously vexed with a devil." How many mothers are there who have to pray this prayer for a child troubled by an evil spirit? In this case it was more sickness than sin, it was the power of Satan in the body more than the soul. How many grown-up children of Christian parents are under the power of Satan, given to pleasure or worldliness, to self-will or to sin? Let our story encourage them to believe that, however hopeless their case appears, there is One who is mighty to save.

Let them come to Him with their need and cry out in prayer, "My child is grievously vexed with a devil." Let them make full confession of their child's lost condition. Beware of excusing their sin by the thought of what is good or loveable about them, or by laying the blame on circumstances or companions. Bring them to Christ and say that they are lost, under the power of Satan. Do not hide their evil condition. Ask not only that they may be saved and made happy and taken to heaven. Ask nothing less than that they may turn from the power of Satan unto God, that they may be translated from the power of darkness to the Kingdom of God's dear Son. Ask that they may be born again, changed from being the children of the devil and the enemies of God to His friends and children.

Her Prayer's Refusal

This is the second lesson this woman has to teach us. Christ seemed to turn a deaf ear to her prayer. At first He did not answer her a word. When He did speak, His answer was worse than

His silence. It cut off all hope: He was not sent to the heathen. She came nearer and again worshipped Him, saying, "Lord, help me!" His second answer appeared to heap contempt on her misfortune: she was not only a heathen, but a dog.

This account gives a true picture of what happens in the heart of many a pleading parent! They hear of Christ's love and power and begin to pray with great urgency, but He answers not a word. There is no sign of thought or change on the part of the lost one. Still they pray, and it is as if the power of sin grows stronger, and the loved one only wanders farther off. Their conscience tells them it is their own parental sin and unworthiness that is to blame. Others may say: how can we expect God to work a miracle for us? Then the parent settles down in quiet despondency and closes his eyes to his own wretchedness. Oh, the dark, heartrending uncertainty as to the salvation of that child!

Her Faith And Perseverance

This mother's example is presented to us because she refused to be denied. She met silence, argument, and contempt with one weapon—more prayer and more trust. She had heard of the wonderful Man and His compassion. She saw the love in His face and heard it in the voice that refused her. She would not believe He would send her away empty. She hoped against hope. She believed against appearances—she believed and she triumphed.

Now, mother, you who are pleading for your prodigal child, you have this woman's example to give you hope. You also have a thousand words of promise and a revelation of the Father's will and the Savior's power that she did not have. Let her faith and perseverance put your unbelief to shame. In the face of all appearances and all doubts, let your faith rise and claim the promise of an answer to prayer in the name of Jesus. Yield yourself to the Holy Spirit and have every doubt brought to the light so you can confess and cast them out. Do not trust in the fervency of your desires or the urgency of your petition. Seek your strength in God's promise and faithfulness, in His power and love. Let your soul, in restful confidence in Jesus, praise Him for His promise and His power to save. In this confidence let nothing shake you from the continuous and persevering prayer of faith. The prayer of faith is always heard.

The Wonderful Blessing

This woman received her daughter's deliverance from this grievous trouble as well as a spiritual blessing—our Lord's delighted approval of her faith: "O woman, great is thy faith! be it unto thee even as thou wilt." Yes, it is in the earnest, believing supplication for a child that the parent's heart can be drawn out toward the Lord. It is then that the parent can learn to know and trust Him.

Mother, if you are pleading for loved ones far from the fold, come nearer to Jesus. He is able, indeed, to save them. He waits for your faith to take hold of His strength, to accept their salvation. Oh, do not let your child perish, because you refuse to come and take time with Him, until His love has inspired you with faith. Mother, come nearer, tarry with Jesus in prayer, trust Him—your child can be saved!

A Parent's Prayer

Lord, I would confess the sin of my child. You know it all: unconverted, and an enemy to You by nature, he has rejected Your love and chosen the world and sin. I confess my sin, too, Lord! You know that, had my life been less in the world and the flesh, purer and holier, more full of faith and of love, my child might have grown up differently. Lord, in deep sorrow I confess my sin. Oh, do not let my child perish. Son of David, have mercy on me. Blessed Lord, I put my trust in You. I look in faith to Your Almighty power. The things that are impossible with man are possible with God. I look in faith to Your promise to hear my prayer. Lord, I believe You hear me. Help my unbelief. I lay this perishing child at Your feet and plead Your love. Savior, I do believe in Your love and claim deliverance for my child. In this faith I will praise You for Your grace. I will wait at Your feet day by day in the rest of faith, praising You and looking for Your fulfillment. Amen.

Chapter 29

KEEPING THE CHILDLIKE SPIRIT

"Whosoever therefore shall humble himself as this little child, the same is greatest in the kingdom of heaven. And whoso shall receive one such little child in my name, receiveth me"—Matthew 18:4,5.

The disciples had come to Jesus with the question, *Who is the greatest in the Kingdom of heaven?* He spoke so often of the Kingdom that to them it suggested the idea of power and glory. They could not but wonder who would have the highest place. How utterly strange and incomprehensible must have been the answer Jesus gave to their question. He called a little child and set him in the midst of them. He told the disciples that as long as they were thinking of who would be greatest, they could not even enter the Kingdom. They must first become as little children, and then the humblest and the most childlike would be the highest in the Kingdom. Whosoever receives one little child in Jesus' name, receives Him. The deeper their likeness to the child-nature, the closer and more complete the union with Himself.

How wonderfully this teaching applies to parents. In creating a family, with father and mother, God sets a little child in their midst. In that little child He opens to them the mystery of the Kingdom of heaven and the spiritual world. He tells them that if they want to know about heaven, and what will equip them for its highest place, they must study the child-nature. On earth they will find nothing so heaven-like as a child, and no surer way to the highest enjoyments of heavenly dignity than in receiving little children in His name. In doing this they will receive Himself in whom the Kingdom is. These are the three lessons we parents must learn.

The Childlike Spirit

What does this mean? Our Savior uses one word, "Whosoever shall *humble* himself as this little child, the same is greatest in the kingdom." The greatest one will be he who thinks least of being greatest, because he loses sight of himself in seeking God and His Kingdom. The great beauty of childlikeness is the absence of self-consciousness. The true child loses himself in that which is around him. The curse of sin is that it makes man, every man, his own focus of attention. Even when he seeks the Kingdom of heaven, he is still thinking how he can be greatest in the Kingdom.

In the true child, self does not yet manifest itself. He lives and is at rest outside of himself in the parent. He loves and rejoices in being loved.

He is honest and trusting toward everyone and expects others to be what they appear. The naturalness and simplicity of a child are closely linked to the traits of the heavenly Kingdom. The lesson we need to learn is that there is nothing a parent should seek to preserve and cherish more carefully than this heavenly childlikeness. It is the secret of that beautiful calmness and serenity which is the image of the peace and restfulness of heaven.

The spirit of the world is the very opposite. With its rivalry and its ambition, it seeks excitement and possessions. Worldliness destroys all that is so beautiful and heavenly in the child, to make way for the self-seeking that are its characteristics. Christian parents are in danger of destroying the simplicity and tenderness of the child-life by stimulating the desires which are of the earth. In the midst of a great deal of Bible teaching and hymn singing, the very heart of true Christianity may be eaten away by the artificial and unchildlike spirit of the homes in which the children are raised.

Parents, make a study to find out what Jesus meant when He spoke so strongly of the need of being childlike. Value the childlikeness and simplicity of your little one as his heavenly beauty. Realize that the little one is sensitive to impressions and alert to all that surrounds him. He will come under the fostering influence of the heavenly life, or the withering effect of a worldly life. There is a wonderful harmony between the Holy

Spirit and the heavenliness of childhood. Train your children in that holy, happy stillness which keeps the child-heart open to the workings of the Holy Spirit.

Childlike Parents

Our Lord's words have a second lesson. If we are to watch over the heavenliness of our children, we must ourselves be childlike and heavenly-minded. Christ put a little child in the midst of strong men to teach them. Parents often owe more to the teaching of their children than they do to them. Our children lose their childlikeness so soon because parents have so little of it. The atmosphere of the home has so little of simple, happy, trustful living in the Father's presence. In many of the social customs of religion, the spirit of the world too often reigns. To be great in the Kingdom of heaven is seldom the goal of most Christians. To be the greatest, as Jesus puts it, by being humble and childlike, the least and the servant of all, this is hardly even considered. No wonder parents, instead of maintaining and strengthening the spirit of the child, hinder and quench it.

Parents must learn to be childlike. There are very few teachings more difficult, yet very few that will bring a richer reward. The little treasures entrusted to us have higher worth than we know. The smallness of children, which we often connect with their weakness, is to Jesus their greatest attraction. It is only the childlike life of the parent, living in great simplicity of truth and trust with the Father in heaven, that can maintain the childlikeness in the child, too.

Receive The Child In Jesus' Name

Let us study the third lesson our Savior teaches: "Whoso receiveth one such little child in My name, receiveth Me." When our children are born we must receive them in the name of Jesus, in His Spirit, with His appreciation of their simplicity and humility. Let us receive them in His name, as those whom He loves and blesses, and of whom He says, "of such is the kingdom." Let us receive them in His name, as sent by Jesus to remind us of His own childlike humility and obedience to the Father. Let us receive them day by day in His name, coming as a gift from the Father. Let us receive them and cherish them in His name, just as He would receive them, as He did receive them, and bless them. Let us receive them in His name, just as we would receive Jesus.

Yes, just as we would receive Jesus. He asks and promises nothing less. "He that receiveth one such little child in My name, receiveth Me." The parent who recognizes and loves the humility of the little child, and on this account receives and treasures the child, receives Christ Himself. This is the promise. With every child something of heaven and of Christ comes into the house. In many cases it is not noticed, not cared for, and the heavenly traits are pushed aside by the world. Blessed are those parents who truly receive the child in Jesus' name, as being from heaven; like heaven and for heaven—they receive Himself. Jesus comes with the little one to be his and their Savior. "Whosoever receiveth one such little child in My name, receiveth Me." With the child He sets in their midst, Jesus takes the parents into His training to teach them how to be great in the Kingdom of heaven. He comes to make their child a blessing to them, so that they may be prepared to be a real blessing to him. He comes to bless parent and child together and make the home what it was meant to be—the picture, the promise, the pathway, to the Father's home in heaven.

Dear Parent, let us ask our Lord Jesus to open our minds to take in His divine thoughts about the heavenliness of our children. Open our eyes to see Him in them, to bring our hearts into perfect sympathy with Himself. May our little ones day by day be the blessed messengers that lead us to heaven, that bring to us Jesus Himself, the life and the light of heaven.

A Parent's Prayer

Lord Jesus, we ask You for a childlike spirit. May the simplicity and peacefulness, the love and the loveliness, the honesty and trust of the child nature dwell in us. In our relationship with our little ones may their heavenly childlikeness not be lost, but cherished and maintained through advancing years. Help us to understand that we can fulfill our parental calling only as we walk with God in childlike simplicity. Blessed Lord, we do thank You that when we receive a child in Your name we receive You as our Teacher and our Helper. We ask You to strengthen us and all parents in this faith. May we understand that You are ready to bless the home where the children are received in Your name, to be saved by You and trained for You. Amen.

Chapter 30

BRING YOUR CHILD TO JESUS

"But Jesus said, Suffer little children, and forbid them not, to come unto Me: for of such is the kingdom of heaven"—Matthew 19:14.

What deep significance there is in this word, "Suffer little children to come unto Me." We suffer, or allow, that which we are not naturally inclined to permit. The mothers of these children had probably heard the words Jesus had just spoken (see Matthew 18:3-5) and brought their little ones to be blessed by this wonderful teacher. Jesus saw the disciples rebuking the mothers. The disciples found it hard to understand and to follow the Master. What could the little children have to do with Him? Jesus hears them and says: Forbid them not; allow them to come unto Me, for of such is the Kingdom of heaven. He loves to have the children around Him because they are nearest to the Kingdom and best suited for it. The Kingdom needs children, as the teachers of the wise and the great, to show the path through which heaven can be entered.

The Child's Faith

"Suffer little children to come unto Me." This word reminds us how our wisdom cannot understand that the Kingdom and the little ones are especially suited for each other. It seems as if the faith of a child is only tolerated—not something to be trusted or rejoiced in. With such a spirit in parents and the Church, it is no wonder that youthful faith is quenched and becomes like that of the majority of older people.

Let parents hear the words of the Master today. If you cannot understand or fully approve, still do not forbid or hinder the children from coming to Jesus. Just be patient until you see how He can bless them. When His word, "of such is the kingdom," has entered your heart, you will learn to receive the children as He did. Only then will you have the right idea of what child-faith is—its nature, its dangers, and its needs.

Child-faith constitutes the very center of God's revelation—coming to Jesus. In His own well-known words, "Come unto Me," our Lord spoke of the blessed rest He would give to all who came to Him to exchange their weary burdens for His loving yoke. This simple gospel is just what a child needs. He is ready to believe in the unseen One, so kind and loving. His humility finds no difficulty in confessing his sins and his need of help. Nothing appears more simple and natural than to obey and follow this loving Savior. Instinctively, the child reconciles faith and works. He sees at once that trust in Jesus should bring about obedience. Above all, the child at once understands what older people often cannot apprehend—that all faith and salvation center in a living Person. To a child, Jesus is loving and to be loved; Jesus is trusted and obeyed; *Jesus, Himself, is Christianity.* If only this could be true throughout our lifetime! Then coming to Jesus in prayer, in surrender, in love, would be the spontaneous exercise of faith. Let us not hinder, but help our children come to Jesus!

Do Not Hinder Them

This faith of a child can be hindered. The words of Jesus suggest this thought. The child is weaker than the older disciple. He is under the elder's influence and can be held back by him. God has given the children into the hands of their elders to be shaped and molded. The natural faith of the child, his sense of love and duty to Jesus, may be terribly hindered by the example and conduct of those around him. Jesus says, "Forbid them not." The word means (as it is elsewhere translated), "Hinder them not." The faith of the child is weak and can easily be hindered. Christian parents are appointed as guardians to watch and foster the growth of the child's faith. All growth comes from within and depends upon a healthy life. Young and feeble growth needs provision for nourishment and preservation from outside danger.

Often parents have been bitterly disappointed in their children. When the children were young, they could feel so deeply and speak so beautifully;

but before long their faith was lost. It is because parents did not watch over the evil influences which the young plant was unable to resist. The parents allowed the spirit of the world into their own spiritual life. They allowed bad company, pleasure, and the enjoyment of the world to choke the good seed. They failed to supply the necessary nourishment. As the child grew up, he no longer spoke in a personal way of this blessed Jesus. His faith and obedience were no longer encouraged by the fellowship and example of a warm, living Christianity, a living love to Jesus. The child's faith disappeared, because the parents hindered him in coming to Jesus.

Bring Them To Jesus

The result is much different when this coming to Jesus is fostered and encouraged not only in the little ones, but in the growing boy and girl during the years that lead to maturity. We must beware of despising a child's spiritual impressions as of little value. Like all beginnings of life and growth, they may be weak and easily lost. However, they are still of infinite value as the preparation for that which will last forever. We must, on the other hand, be kept from over-estimating their impressions. We must remember that the tender child needs unceasing watching. Only in the happy atmosphere of a holy home can we expect fruit to ripen into eternal life.

We have already suggested what a child's faith needs. Just permit the child to come to Jesus and remove every hindrance. Believe deeply what Jesus says, "of such is the kingdom," and allow this heavenly element in the child's nature to show itself and to reach out after the Son of God. Make it your chief aim to teach the child about Jesus and encourage him to come to Him to be saved from sin. Beware of coming between the child and Jesus. Let the child under your leading have free access to Jesus. Beware of hindering him by distrust or disinterest. Let the child see the warmth of your love for Jesus, your holy example of obedience, your teaching and praying. Let your whole life daily help the child to see Jesus, to live with Him, and to long for Him. Jesus Christ is meant to be our everyday friend, our every hour companion. Let all the influence you possess in forming your child and fixing his destiny be used for this one thing—to satisfy the desire of the Savior's heart and make your child His.

These words of Christ's were spoken to disciples who knew Him and confessed Him as the Son of God. They were sound in the faith, Christ's chosen friends. However, they did not understand His thoughts about the children. This thought was too high for them, because the love of childlikeness is one of the highest things in the Kingdom. Many a theologian, preacher, and parent is not yet in sympathy with Jesus' feelings about children. Dear parents who have taken the Savior as your only teacher, let Him teach you the preciousness of your little ones. Learn to see in them what He does. Then, in His light, your care of them will become a blessing to yourself and to them.

A Parent's Prayer

Blessed Savior, again we ask You to open our eyes to see in our little ones what You see. Help us to think of them as You do, as belonging to You and the Kingdom. We ask, Lord, for heavenly wisdom to know how to guide them in coming to You and to help them to abide with You. Teach us to see a child's impressions as the seeds of eternal life. May our faith in Your love for them be the power by which their young hearts are made strong. Grant us Your Holy Spirit that, day by day and year by year, we may possess and train them for You alone and for Your glory. Amen.

Chapter 31

YOUR FAITH AND YOUR CHILD'S
SALVATION

"And straightway the father of the child cried out, and said with tears, Lord, I believe; help thou mine unbelief"—Mark 9:24.

When Jesus spoke to the disciples about the mothers who were coming with their little children to Him, His word was, "Suffer the little children, and forbid them not to come unto Me" (Matthew 19:14). In this story He uses a stronger word. When the father of the lunatic boy told Jesus that the disciples had not been able to cast out the evil spirit, He reproved them for their unbelief. He said to them, *"Bring* the child unto Me." This expression is a stronger one, still setting forth the same truth. The little ones were quite ready and willing to come to the loving Stranger to be blessed. This poor boy, at times unconscious, had to be brought whether he knew it or not. There can be no evil spirit in a child so strong—no resistance so desperate—that can violate the parent's liberty and power to bring him to Jesus. To every disciple, to every father and mother, in every crisis of sin or need, Christ's voice is heard calling, "Bring the child unto Me."

The Importance Of Faith

If we want to understand what it means to bring a child on whom Satan has a hold to Jesus, we can study the conversation between this father and Jesus. In answer to Christ's question, the father told the touching story of how the boy had been the prey of this terrible trouble ever since his childhood. The father had pleadingly added, "If Thou canst do anything, have compassion on us and help us." Jesus threw all the responsibility upon the father and said, "If thou canst believe, all things are possible to him that believeth" (see Mark 9:22-23). It was not a question of whether Jesus could and would do it, but whether the father could believe. If he did, the healing was sure. If he did not believe, the healing could not take place.

"If thou canst believe, all things are possible to him that believeth." These words are one of the well-known expressions in which all the blessings of God's mighty, saving love are put at the disposal of faith. By faith we understand both what God has done and will do. We look to God to do what He has promised, and so give Him the glory. Faith is yielding our will to God's holy will to take possession of us and work out His pleasure. "All things are possible to him that believeth," because "with God nothing shall be impossible," and faith is union with God (see Luke 1:37).

In speaking these words to the father of the lunatic, Jesus gave to us, for all time, the secret of successful parental training and prayer. He tells us that it is not only the ministers of His gospel, but every Christian parent who needs to exercise strong faith. Using his strong faith, the parent can secure the salvation of his child. His compassion and power are longing to help us, if we can believe. If not, we are to blame if our children perish.

The Parent's Unbelief

Most parents seek the cause of unconverted and unsaved children in God—not in themselves. Has God's sovereignty nothing to do with the salvation of our children? Is there not such a thing as election? If so, how can all the responsibility be thrown on our unbelief? Scripture reveals to us most clearly God's sovereignty. His grace is electing grace. The final decision of the destiny of each man is in His hands. Scripture reveals, just as clearly, man's responsibility and all-prevailing power of faith. True humility accepts both statements without reconciling them. It bows under the solemn truth Jesus utters here that, if the parent can believe, the child can be saved.

Our text tells us how this truth ought to affect us. With tears the father cried, "Lord, I believe, help mine unbelief." He was in agony to think that his unbelief might keep the blessing from his child. The father bursts into tears, casts himself at

Jesus' feet to confess his unbelief, and asks deliverance from it. It is amid these tears of repentance and confession that the father's faith is exercised and the victory is given. The devil is cast out, and the child is saved. Christ's heart-searching word to the father had revealed his unbelief and awakened the faith that brought the blessing.

Christ's word must do the same with every parent, with every father, who pleads for a child's liberation from Satan's power. A father's tears have power. There must be confession and humbling wherever there is strong faith. There must be the conviction and confession of the sin of unbelief. The parent must confess that this has been the cause of the blessing being withheld, and that he is guilty of not believing.

When the disciples asked the Master why they could not cast out this devil, He told them it was because of their unbelief. This unbelief was caused by their life not being one of prayer and fasting. Unbelief is not, as many think, an unexplainable weakness that is beyond our power. Unbelief has its reasons: it is the indication of the state of heart. The worldly person cannot believe. The self-righteous, the proud man, cannot believe. It is only the pure in heart, the humble, the soul that thirsts for God and forsakes all to follow Christ, who can be strong in faith. Therefore, the first step in the path of an overcoming faith is the confession of sinfulness.

Confess Your Unbelief

I have heard parents plead very earnestly with God for the conversion of their grown-up children, when I secretly feared that their prayers would not be heard. I saw no sign of confession of parental sin. There are parents whose worldliness, whose lack of living faith, whose self-indulgence, and whose neglect in the education of their children, have simply sown the seeds which they are now reaping in the departure of their children from God. Yet, they wonder why their children are not more religious. They sometimes pray earnestly for them and try to have faith that their children will be saved. They may be deceiving themselves. True faith sanctifies. It searches the heart. It confesses the sin of unbelief, along with its root and strength. True faith casts itself weeping and helpless at the feet of Jesus. There, and there alone, bowing in its weakness, resting on His strength, faith obtains the blessing He loves to bestow.

Fathers who would like to bring their sons to Jesus to be saved, come and hear the lessons the Lord wants to teach you. Let these children first bring you to Jesus in confession, prayer, and trust. Your faith can then bring them in truth. In yourself, and in them, you will experience what the all-prevailing power and truth is of the word: "If thou canst believe, all things are possible to him that believeth."

A Parent's Prayer

Blessed Son of God, look in mercy upon a parent who now comes to You with a child still unconverted and under the power of the evil one. Lord Jesus, have compassion on us and help us! Let this child be delivered from Satan's power and make him a child of God. I have to confess how little my life has been a life of faith, and how my unbelief has hindered the blessing from my child. I have to confess the worldliness, selfishness, and the lack of entire surrender and obedience to You which has made strong faith impossible. Lord, I believe! Help my unbelief. I look to Your Word and hold firmly to it. I yield myself to a life of entire surrender to You, to be Yours alone. Blessed Lord Jesus, I do believe that You hear and save my child. In this faith I praise Your holy name. Amen.

Chapter 32

THE EXPECTANT MOTHER

"He shall be filled with the Holy Ghost, even from his mother's womb" —Luke 1:15.

May God grant us His grace to meditate on the truth revealed to us in this verse. This truth is very precious to a believing parent: *the mother's womb is the work place of the Holy Spirit.* Our Lord has taught us that the least in the Kingdom of heaven is greater than John the Baptist. If he was filled with the Holy Spirit from before his birth, how much more can the child of believing parents also be filled.

We find here, at the very opening of New Testament history, the same truth that we learned in studying God's covenant with the patriarchs. In preparing and securing servants to do His work, God loves to begin at the very beginning. From before the birth, from the very first conception of life, God begins to sanctify the vessel He is to use for His service. The more distinctly we understand this part of God's plan with His people, the better we will understand the holy privilege of being a parent. Mothers especially will be encouraged and strengthened in faith to yield themselves, with all the hopes and joys of motherhood, to be God's chosen vessels for the fulfillment of His purpose and the perfecting of His Church.

God Seeks Holy Parents

Let us look first at what Scripture teaches about the parents in whom the Holy Spirit is thus to work. Of John's parents it is testified: "They were both righteous before God, walking in all the commandments and ordinances of the Lord blameless" (Luke 1:6).

It is the God of nature, who in this world of cause and effect has ordered that like produces like. God has all power and can work any miracle He pleases, yet He most carefully observes His own laws. When He wants a holy child, God seeks for holy parents. Throughout Scripture, especially in the New Testament, the blessed indwelling of the Holy Spirit is promised to the obedient. Man must, in obedience to divine command, prepare his heart. Then the Holy Spirit comes to take possession and fill it.

God chose parents who were walking blameless in all the commandments and ordinances of the Lord. Their child was to be the forerunner of the Savior, filled with the Holy Spirit from his mother's womb. It is of holy parents that God forms a holy child.

The Mother's Holy Calling

The double lesson for every parent, and especially for every mother, is of deepest interest. A righteous and blameless life prepares for the power of the Holy Spirit to indwell the unborn child. Let expectant mothers, who would fulfill their holy calling as the ministers of their Lord's purposes, study Elizabeth's character: "righteous, and walking in all the commandments of the Lord *blameless.*" It is to such a life that God chose us, "that we should be holy and *without blame* before Him in love" (Ephesians 1:4). It is to such a life Jesus redeemed us: "He hath reconciled you in the body of His flesh through death, to present you holy and *unblameable* and unreprovable in His sight" (Colossians 1:21,22). This is no more than what every child of God ought to be and can be, "*blameless* and harmless. . .without rebuke, in the crooked and perverse generation" (Philippians 2:15). Every expectant mother should offer her body as the temple of the Holy Spirit, so that the very beginning of life in her may be overshadowed by the Holy Spirit.

Oh, that mothers, and fathers, too, understood how terribly the spirit of the world and the flesh affects their unborn child. A life in which sin and selfishness are allowed to have rule hinders the influence of the Spirit. It can cause the child to inherit unholy appetites and passions.

Parents must realize that a life which seeks to walk in obedience and righteousness, blameless before the Lord, will be accepted and honored by Him. Godly parents have a right to ask and confidently expect the Spirit in them to take possession of the life God gives through them. Let them cherish this as the highest and the brightest hope of holy motherhood: "He shall be filled with the Holy Ghost, even from his mother's womb."

The Spirit-born Child

Let us now look at what the angel's message teaches us *of the child* who is born to godly parents. "Thou shalt have joy and gladness; and many shall rejoice at his birth, for he shall be great in the sight of the Lord" (Luke 1:14,15). These are the characteristics of a child born under the covering of the Holy Spirit. The parents are to "have joy and gladness." How many Christian parents have had reason to say in bitter agony, Would to God my child had never been born! Do you want divinely given joy and gladness in the children who are given you? Then let the Holy Spirit take possession of them from before their birth. You will have the holy joy of heaven as you see the beauty of the Lord upon them. It will be a joy that no one can take away.

"And many shall rejoice at his birth." How many children of Christian parents have been the curse of their fellow-men! Do you want many people to thank God that your child was born? Study the story of John's birth. Study it in connection with the story of Jesus' birth. It was in virtue of his connection with Jesus that John was filled with the

Holy Spirit from his mother's womb. Claim the outpouring of the Spirit upon all flesh and the promise of the Spirit to you and your children. Then your faith will be strengthened to believe that your child, too, will be filled with the Spirit and make many rejoice at his birth.

"For he shall be great in the sight of the Lord" (Luke 1:15). A joy to his parents, a blessing to his fellow-men, and great in the sight of the Lord, is the Spirit-born child. Among men he may not be famous, in gifts and talents he may not be great; but he will be great in the sight of Him who does not see as man sees. He will be a vessel God can use for His work, a true way-preparer for the coming of the Lord and His Kingdom.

Mother, God gives you this picture of Elizabeth and her child of promise, with the double lesson: live as she did; believe and receive what she did. Young mother, your motherhood is in God's sight a holier and more blessed thing than you know. If you are indeed God's child, you have in everything been placed under the leading and the rule of His Holy Spirit. Be sure that all the tender interest, all the quiet trust and joyful hope which expectant motherhood calls forth, is sanctified and refined by God's Holy Spirit. Then you will be united with your little one under the overshadowing of His heavenly grace.

A Parent's Prayer

Blessed God, what a deep interest You have in developing holy and blameless mothers. You call her to live a righteous and blameless life to do her holy work. You teach her that the life she is to bring forth is a holy gift from You, to be received and carried in a pure and holy vessel. Great and glorious God, in deep humility and trembling, Your handmaid bows before You to offer herself to Your service. O my Father, give Your Holy Spirit to Your children to make them Your temple. Fulfill Your wonderful promise to Your child. Let Your Holy Spirit dwell in me. If it please You to make me the mother of a child, let him be filled with the Spirit from the womb. Let me be filled with the Spirit. Let my child be born only for this one thing, that he may be great in Your sight and a blessing to all around him. Amen.

Chapter 33

A MOTHER'S SURRENDER

"And Mary said, Behold the handmaid of the Lord; be it unto me according to thy word"— Luke 1:38.

We have often had occasion to notice the wonderful oneness of mother and child. We see to what extent the mother, in her life and character, influences and decides what the child is to be. The life she imparts is her own life, in the deepest meaning of the term. When God gave His Son to be born of a woman, this law was not violated. The mother He chose for His Son was, doubtless, all that grace could make her to be. She was the chosen vessel through whom He would receive His human nature and character.

Mary's Example Of Faith

Just as Jesus is in everything our example, so we may naturally expect that, in His mother, God has given us an example for mothers. If the child Jesus is an example for our children, there will also be something for mothers to learn from His mother.

The heavenly messenger said to Mary, "Hail thou, highly favoured, the Lord is with thee: blessed art thou among women" (Luke 1:28). Her cousin Elizabeth, filled with the Holy Spirit, also said to Mary, "Blessed art thou among women, and blessed is the fruit of thy womb. . . .and blessed is she that believed" (Luke 1:42,45). Her words and ways have left an example for every mother who yields herself like Mary to the Lord, to bear a child that can be called a son of the Most High. If there were more mothers like Mary, there would be more children like the holy Child Jesus.

What constitutes the most marked feature of Mary's motherhood? It is the childlike simplicity of faith in which she surrenders herself to the divine purpose: "Behold the handmaid of the Lord; be it unto me according to Thy word." She calls herself the Lord's slave or bondwoman; she gives her will, herself, up to Him, to do what pleases Him. In quiet trust and expectancy she looks to Him to do what He has said. The same spirit of obedient faith which equipped Abraham to be the father of the promised seed, now prepares her to become the mother of Him in whom the promise is to be fulfilled.

There were, however, still difficulties and questions. When the angel appeared to Mary, "she was troubled at his saying, and cast in her mind what manner of salutation this should be" (Luke 1:29). When again he had spoken, she questioned, "How shall this be, seeing I know not a man?" (Luke 1:34). When once the angel had spoken to her of the power of the Most High overshadowing her, she yielded herself to the divine word. She became an example to every mother who would share the benediction, "Blessed is she that believed for there shall be a performance of those things which were told her from the Lord" (Luke 1:45). It is the surrender of faith that blesses motherhood: "Blessed art thou, and blessed is the fruit of thy womb."

The Yielded And Trusting Mother

"Behold the handmaid of the Lord." Mary teaches a mother to yield herself to God for the service of His Kingdom. In her, His purpose and glory may be made manifest. The birth of each of our children under God's guardianship is a link in the golden chain of the good pleasure of God's will.

Over all the impulses of human love and the instincts of a God-given maternity, there hovers a divine purpose using them for the carrying out of His plan. The life of the wife and mother will take on new meaning when she realizes herself to be the Lord's bondwoman from whom may be born a generation to serve the Lord. Then human love receives divine consecration. What appears to be only natural and earthly is elevated into the heavenlies. Then the expectant mother sees herself like the angels, one of His servants, doing His commandments, hearkening unto the voice of His word.

"Be it unto me according to Thy word." Such is

the faith that gives the strength to surrender one-self to God's service. It looks no longer at difficulties or impossibilities, but it counts upon God to carry out His purpose and to give grace and strength for the work to which He has called us. It is just this faith that, above everything, equips us for the blessed duties of motherhood. Faith gives that quiet rest of body and spirit which to mother and babe is health and strength.

What mother is there who, when she first becomes aware of her new vocation, is not at times with Mary greatly troubled and asks the question, "How can all this be?" She finds no rest so sure or sweet as to cast her troubles on her Lord—let Him do what seemeth to Him good. If the God of nature has created her to fulfill that calling in the interests of His Kingdom, she can trust His power and love not to forsake her in her hour of need. "What time I am afraid, I will trust in Thee. . .in God I have put my trust; I will not fear" (Psalm 56:3,4). Such words have a thousand times over been the comfort of the trembling, but trusting, handmaid of the Lord.

Pondering God's Word

To understand fully the teaching of Mary's example, there is one trait of her character we must study. Twice it is said of her, "Mary kept all these things, and pondered them in her heart" (see Luke 2:19, 51). It is in moments of quiet meditation and reflection on what God has said that the spirit of trust is cultivated. It is only as

God's words are kept and pondered in the heart that they can quicken and deepen a living faith in Him who speaks them. Every mother who searches Holy Scripture will find many verses referring to her sacred calling which will fill her heart with confidence and joy. They will teach her to regard everything connected with the birth of the child as a matter of deepest interest to the Father in heaven and of great importance to His Kingdom.

She will see how all the exceeding great and precious promises may be claimed by her for the little one, even before he has seen the light. She will see how her receiving the little one in the name of Jesus has the promise of Jesus' presence for herself and for her child. She will find that all training of the child has been provided for in regulations of divine wisdom and love. She will discover that all the grace needed for carrying out these orders is most surely given to each mother. Like Mary, she will be a bondmaid of the Lord and will believe what He has spoken. All care and fear, danger and pain, joy and rich reward God has connected with the life of motherhood—all is written in the Book of the Lord. The mother who listens, waits, and believes will be able to say, "Behold the handmaid of the Lord; be it unto me according *to Thy word*." As she waits for the birth of the child and ponders God's words, she will find how true the word is, "*Blessed* is she that believed."

Forming The Mother's Character

What a holy and blessed thing the birth of a

child becomes in the light of the birth of Jesus! What a holy and blessed calling the mother's task becomes in the light of the favor of the Most High God. It becomes the means of the fulfillment of His purpose, the promotion of His glory, and the experience of His special grace and mercy!

As the mother ponders these things, she will understand something of the deep meaning of that word of Paul, "She shall be saved in childbearing, if they continue in faith and charity and holiness with sobriety" (1 Timothy 2:15). Just as labor by the sweat of his brow was given to man in his fallen state, so the labor of childbearing was given to the woman. Through it and its blessed discipline, the life of Christ can more effectually be accomplished in her whole character. Childbearing helps produce in the mother that blessed life of faith, trust, love, gentleness, motherly kindness, holiness, and self-control. It helps to form that perfect womanly character which is one of God's most beautiful gifts on earth.

In this path of loving acceptance of God's appointment and trustful resting in His promise, this word will come true for each expectant mother: "Blessed art thou, and blessed is the fruit of thy womb."

A Parent's Prayer

Lord, teach me to look upon everything connected with the birth of my child as of deepest interest to my Father. Help me to cast every fear and burden, every care and pain, on Him in whose service these come. In childlike faith, O my Lord, I would take Your blessed Word, with all its teachings and its promises, as my light and strength. In the time of patient waiting or in the hour of anguish, Your Word shall be my comfort. Unfold the treasures Your Word contains for me as a mother, that I may know at the right time to receive what You have provided. Behold the handmaid of the Lord; be it unto me according to Your Word. Amen.

Chapter 34

A MOTHER'S JOY

"And Mary said, My soul doth magnify the Lord, and my spirit hath rejoiced in God my Saviour. For He hath regarded the low estate of His handmaiden" —Luke 1:46-48.

There is perhaps no moment of greater joy or thanksgiving than when a woman knows she is the mother of a living child. Our blessed Lord compared this joy of motherhood with the joy of resurrection: "A woman when she is in travail hath sorrow, because her hour is come: but as soon as she is delivered of the child, she remembereth no more the anguish, for joy that a man is born into the world" (John 16:21). A mother will not find a more perfect expression for her joy than in thanksgiving to Him to whom she owes so much.

Using God's Word To Thank Him

In many portions of Holy Scripture, a mother will find the most suitable language to express her thanks to God. How often, for instance, has the mother almost instinctively spoken the words of

Psalm 103: "Bless the Lord, O my soul; and all that is within me, bless His holy name. Bless the Lord, O my soul, and forget not all His benefits: who forgiveth all thine iniquities; who healeth all thy diseases; who redeemeth thy life from destruction; who crowneth thee with lovingkindness and with tender mercies; who satisfieth thy mouth with good things; so that thy youth is renewed like the eagle's" (verses 1-5). After the birth of the little one, the Lord would like to keep the mother for a little while in the secret place of His Holy presence, to encourage and instruct her for the solemn responsibilities awaiting her. Nothing will be more pleasing to her Lord and more refreshing and strengthening for her own life. The spirit of thanksgiving should give its bright tone to all her thoughts and hopes. This song of praise should be repeated day by day: "My soul doth magnify the Lord, and my spirit hath rejoiced in God my Saviour. For He hath regarded the low estate of His handmaiden. . . For He that is mighty hath done to me great things, and holy is His name; and His mercy is on them that fear Him, from generation to generation" (Luke 1:46-50).

Reasons For Giving Thanks

It is hardly necessary to remind a mother of all there is to stir her to praise. She has only to think of the anxious thoughts and fears that would sometimes come up as the solemn hour of her trial rose up before her, and her song is, "I sought the Lord, and He heard me, and delivered me from all my fears" (Psalm 34:4). She looks at the precious little treasure that has been given her, with all the love and joy he brings into her heart and home, and the words come spontaneously: "What shall I render to the Lord for all His benefits toward me?" (Psalm 116:12).

She sees in the little one, as she looks upon him in the light of God's purpose and promise, an immortal being. He was created to show forth God's glory on earth and share that glory in heaven, as a jewel in Jesus' crown. Her soul bows in trembling wonder at the thought of keeping and forming such a treasure. She remembers that the little one has inherited from her an evil nature, yet through her he also has the promise of the covenant and the Spirit. Her child is holy, because she is one of God's holy ones in Christ. She thinks of all the grace, wisdom, and strength He has provided for her so that she can secure all that God's love has prepared.

She listens to the voice, "My grace is sufficient for thee: my strength is made perfect in weakness" (2 Corinthians 12:9). Then she can only sing again, "My soul doth magnify *the Lord*, and my spirit doth rejoice *in God my Saviour*. . .His mercy is on them that fear Him, from generation to generation." *It is God Himself* in whom Mary, in whom the believer, in whom the grateful mother, is glad and rejoices.

Thanksgiving And Duty

This spirit of thanksgiving, in which we rejoice

in Him, is of greater value than can be expressed. It lifts all out of the sphere of nature and into the fellowship of the spiritual and the divine. In this way it is the true preparation for all the work the mother has before her.

We saw in Mary's giving of herself to her God the two elements of surrender and trust. She surrendered to the work she had to perform, "Behold the bondmaid of the Lord." She trusted God to do for her what He had promised, "Be it according to Thy word." Thanksgiving and joy in the hour of deliverance, if cultivated and kept up, will bring guidance and strength.

"Behold the handmaid of the Lord." The labor of bearing a child is only the beginning of that labor of love to which God has appointed the mother. The whole work of raising, guarding, and training the child is to follow. The spirit of thanksgiving is the best preparation for the altar of consecration. If the mother is indeed to receive grace for the successful fulfillment of this new responsibility, she must give herself to be the Lord's willing, loving slave for this holy work. She must realize that there may be much that has to be put away, much that she will have to struggle against and overcome, to be the holy mother of a holy child.

However, the thought may come that the sacrifice and the strain will be too great, that it is impossible to live so strictly, entirely, and peculiarly given up to God's service. We are afraid of being different from others. We want God to bless us and our children even though we are not so very holy. If such thoughts come, each mother should just pause and think of what God has done! There is the new life given to herself and her precious little one. There is the love and mercy of God and the promise of more love and mercy to be poured out.

If her thanksgiving has been sincere, it will lead the mother to say that she will live for God and that she will train her child to be the Lord's. "The joy of the Lord is your strength" (Nehemiah 8:10). A mother's joy is the power for a mother's work. The spirit of thanksgiving leads to the altar of consecration where mother and child are laid as living sacrifices to be the Lord's alone.

"Be it unto me according to Thy word." This word of faith and trust, looking to God to do all that He has promised, gets new meaning after the experience of the first part of its fulfillment. Let the mother yield herself heartily, not to her work, but to her God for Him to work. She may depend upon the fact that His teaching, His help, and His strength are realities. Let her, in the joyful spirit of praise, take His Word and note what it says of the Father in heaven and the abounding grace He has undertaken to supply.

The joy of a child born into the world is just the beginning of a joy that shall know no ending. Let thanksgiving lift the heart to God in praise. Then faith becomes easy; thanksgiving becomes natural; and the life of mother and child become one unceasing song of faith and love, of surrender and obedience, of thanksgiving and praise.

A Parent's Prayer

Father, hear the prayer of Your handmaid and let my life indeed become new. In close fellowship with my Lord Jesus, in a very tender yielding to the leading of the Holy Spirit, I desire to live only and completely as Your handmaid. Lord, I offer You my precious child. Make me worthy to keep this child as a sacred trust from You to nurse and train as Yours. Let me know that You have accepted me and my little one to keep as Your own for evermore. Amen.

Chapter 35

A CHILD LIKE JESUS

"They brought Him to Jerusalem, to present Him to the Lord, (as it is written in the law of the Lord, Every male that openeth the womb shall be called holy to the Lord;) and to offer a sacrifice according to that which is said in the law of the Lord"—Luke 2:22-24.

According to the law of God in Israel, a child was circumcised when eight days old. This was done in the home. On the fortieth day the mother was to appear in the temple to bring the sacrifice of her purification and to present her child to the Lord. If the child was a firstborn, then his presentation had special reference to the firstborn belonging to the Lord. He had to be redeemed. The Child Jesus also had to be presented to the Lord as being made like unto His brethren in all things under the law. Made like us in all things, not only that He might have experience of everything we pass through, but that we might know that every condition has been sanctified by His Holy Presence. When we pass through these experiences, He imparts to us the blessing that flows from fellowship with Him. This truth brings joy and comfort for parents as they bring their little ones to be dedicated to the Lord.

Presenting Your Child To The Lord

Let us study this presentation of the holy Child Jesus in the Temple. He is presented to His Father in heaven by His earthly parents; a helpless infant, but yet a pleasing sacrifice, a sweet-smelling savor. He also comes as the firstborn among many brethren, the forerunner, through whom our little ones can also be accepted by the Holy One. When we bring our child to present him to the Lord, God looks down from heaven on the offering and gives to our child the spirit of His holy childhood. He was, indeed, made like us, that we might become like Him. He was made like unto our children, that they might be made like Him. He was not only Mary's firstborn, but the Father's firstborn among many brethren.

Where the first fruits are holy, the whole family is holy. The presentation of the Child Jesus to the Father gives us a right to present our children as acceptable, too. I can place my child beside the holy Child and, in faith, claim that in Him my child is also holy and accepted.

In Israel the presentation of the child was accompanied with a sacrifice to cleanse away the defilement of sin cleaving, at every birth, to both mother and child. We need this cleansing, too. The mother can now look to the blessed Jesus, the great sin-offering and atonement (see Leviticus 12:6), for her cleansing from all sin. In this way, she is accepted and equipped for being a true mother to this God-devoted child! The children, too, share in the results of that great sacrifice even before they know it! From their birth they now are holy to the Lord. They may receive that Holy Spirit which is the lawful inheritance of the seed of God's believing people. We present our little one to the Lord, with Jesus as the great sin-offering making us acceptable, clean, and holy to the Lord.

What we present to God "as it is written in the law of the Lord," God takes. What He takes, He keeps. Our faith has only to look to God's taking and keeping to have the joyful assurance that the matter is finally settled between God and us. Let this faith make you strong to train the child for God in strength and grace. He will give this faith to secure His property for Himself. Let this faith speak to your child, as he can receive it: he has been presented with Jesus, like Jesus, in Jesus, to the Father. Let the holy childhood of Jesus overshadow and sanctify the childhood of your little one. Let your children grow up in the friendship and the footsteps of the holy Child.

Your Child, Like Jesus

Live in everything as those who are going to train children who are to be like Jesus. If the thought seems too high, ask the Father whether He does desire your child to be like His. Ask whether He does expect you to train him to be like Jesus.

The answer will not be withheld. The presentation of Jesus in the temple will enable you to see how Jesus is the promise of what your child can be. It will help you to train him accordingly.

In this chapter we have been meditating on spiritual things and speaking less of the practical training in daily life. Let parents be assured that there is nothing more intensely practical than an act of real faith. If our presenting a child to the Lord is a deed of an intelligent, childlike, heartfelt faith, it will influence our daily treatment of the child. If we daily dedicate our child to the Lord, every part of our relationship with him will be affected.

God never would expect us to take charge of an immortal spirit without providing the grace to do it well. As we give ourselves to a life of consecration and holiness, our faith will be the vital principle ruling all our conduct. Our faith will sanctify our home life and elevate our training to what God would have it to be. Our faith will transform each child who, like Jesus, has been presented to Him. Our children will be transformed into the likeness of the life of Him who is the firstborn among many brethren.

A Parent's Prayer

Eternal God, the Father of our Lord Jesus Christ, we draw near to You with our little one to present him to the Lord. We bring our child to You to cleanse from the sin he has inherited through birth from sinful parents. Accept this child as Your own to be set apart and sealed as holy to the Lord. We present this child to You, O Lord God. We do so with the assurance of faith and hope, because Your own holy Child Jesus was once presented on behalf of all children brought to You in faith. Blessed God, beside Him, and in Him, we present our child unto the Lord. We ask You to help us understand all that Your Son's being made like our children implies. Let the likeness of our child to Your child Jesus, be the beginning of a likeness that will take possession of his life. Give grace to Your servants to be the worthy parents and guardians of a child who has been presented to the Lord, as Jesus was. Amen.

Chapter 36

FAITH IN THE HOME

"There cometh one from the ruler of the synagogue's house, saying to Him, Thy daughter is dead; trouble not the Master. But when Jesus heard it, He answered him, saying, Fear not; believe only, and she shall be made whole"— Luke 8:49,50.

Fear not, only believe! To many thousands that word has been the messenger of comfort and hope. As they struggled under the burden of sin or sought for help in trial or difficulty, it told them that there was deliverance from fear by believing in Jesus! Faith can banish fear. Yet, many who have found a blessing in this word have forgotten that it is a word that especially belongs to parents. In every other use it is only a loan, but as parents we have full right to it. It is Jesus, the Lord of parents and children, who speaks: Fear not, only believe. This word reminds us of the double lesson—in our children there is every reason for fear, in Jesus every reason for faith.

Reasons For Fear

When we look at our children, there is every cause for fear. When we think of the evil nature they inherit from us and the mighty power Satan has in this world into which they are entering, we should be afraid. When we see, both in Scripture and in the world around us, how often the children of a religious home depart into the ways of evil and of death, we should fear. When we think of the dangers to which they often are exposed, in the little friends of their childhood, in the schools through which they must pass, we should be alarmed. When we think of the spirit of the world with which they must come into contact, in the literature, the amusements, and the business from which they cannot be kept separate, we should be frightened.

When we think of our children and realize how weak and unfaithful we are to take care of them, the fear grows stronger. We know how the atmosphere we create and breathe through our home is stronger than all precept or external practice. We are deeply aware of how much worldliness and selfishness there is in us. We lack the fullness of the Spirit and the love of God. We tremble at the thought of how our children could suffer from our lack of grace.

Reasons For Faith

To such parents the word of Jesus is given: Fear not, only believe. Only believe: for faith is the one condition through which the power and the salvation of God are given. Only believe: for it is by faith that we throw ourselves and our children on Jesus and secure His blessing. Only believe: let faith look upon God's covenant with us and our seed as He desires to give parents and children His grace. Only believe: it is faith that is the mighty renewing power in a man's life that teaches him to obey and do all that God has commanded. Only believe: this is the one thing Jesus asks of the parent who truly seeks his child's deliverance from sin and death.

A Christian parent's first duty is faith. Just as with the penitent sinner, or the believer seeking more grace, all things are possible to him who believes. Our domestic, as well as our personal life, must be a life of faith. We must not only have the heart, but the home, too, purified by faith. Faith is the one thing God asks for in His children. Parental faith is the only source of parental duty, obedience, happiness, and blessing. "Only believe" must be written on the doorposts of our homes. It must be the motivating power of all we are and do for our children. It must be, in the fullest sense of the word, our only care and aim: Jesus said, Only believe.

God's Word And Faith

To realize this truth, it may be well to remember what God's Word says of faith and its results. In Hebrews, chapter eleven, we read: faith understands; faith offers a more excellent sacrifice; faith pleases God; faith saves the household; faith obeys when it is called; faith receives strength to bear a child; faith offers up the child; faith blesses the children; faith hides the little one; faith saves the firstborn. Faith is first the spiritual understanding that receives the revelation of God and His purpose.

Faith hears His voice, listens to His call, and believes His promises. It is a divine energy, a living principle of action that carries out God's will and inherits all His blessing. It is especially the parent's grace we see in what is said of Noah, Abraham, Sarah, Jacob, Moses' parents, and Moses. It was in each case faith that made it possible, simple, and easy. As parents, it was faith that made them the channels of a divine blessing to their children.

The power to understand God's purpose with our children, to save our household, to obey God's will, to offer our children to God, to bless our sons, and to save them from the destroyer, depends upon our faith. The living Christ is our salvation and our strength. It is in the knowledge of who He is, and in His presence, that such a faith is possible.

Has He not redeemed our children as well as ourselves from the power of sin? Has He not come to make the covenant of promise, "Thy God and the God of thy house," a brighter and fuller reality than ever it was to Abraham? Has He not secured for us, in the Holy Spirit, a power from on high to fulfill our obligation of keeping our children for

Him to whom we belong? Has He not made true all the promises given of old, in that one word on the day of Pentecost, "the promise is to you and to your children"? Can we not count upon Him to give for us and each child just what we need, if only we believe?

The Parents' Living Faith

"Only believe." Let us take the command literally. Faith has never yet been disappointed. Living faith will teach us to see new beauty and preciousness in our children. Living faith will awaken in us new earnestness and desire to train them for God alone. Living faith will give its own hopeful tone to our relationship with God and with our children. The birth of our children, our love for them, our prayers with and for them, our watching against their sins and reproving them, our teaching and training—all will be under the inspiring and regulating power of this: Only believe.

Such a faith life in the home is not possible without the faith life in the heart. We cannot be to our children more than we are to God. "I live; yet not I, but Christ liveth in me. . .I live by the faith of the Son of God" (Galatians 2:20). This must be the language of the father and the mother who would have their house be a home of faith. It is not only in a moment of special need and prayer, or when we are in direct contact with the children, that Jesus says, Only believe. No, day by day, hour by hour, it must be—I live by the faith of the Son of God.

Christian parent, this life is for you. Learn with each new morning to say: For this day I accept Jesus for all my duties as believer and as parent. Commit to Him every duty, every difficulty, every circumstance, every moment. Say confidently, I know in whom I have believed. It is He who spoke to me as a parent the blessed word, Only believe, and I am persuaded that what I have committed to Him He is able to keep. This is the blessed secret of a faith life and a faith home.

A Parent's Prayer

Lord, I ask You to teach me and all parents how impossible it is to properly train our children or be a blessing to them, except as we live the life of faith. Open our eyes to see how our love for them, our influence on them, our training, may all be inspired and perfected by faith in the power of Your abiding presence. Our fears, our children's disobedience, and the wickedness in the world, can be fully met by Your power and Your love, if we only trust You. Lord Jesus, teach us to know You as the Savior of our children from their very birth. Let our whole life and relationship with them, every day and all day, be in the faith of the Son of God, who loved us and gave Himself for us. Amen.

Chapter 37

WHEN A CHILD DIES

"And all wept, and bewailed her: but (Jesus) said, Weep not; she is not dead, but sleepeth"—Luke 8:52.

In God's great school of tribulation there are many classes. In the section where God trains parents, there is one room which everyone greatly fears to enter. Many, as they are led into it, are seen struggling and murmuring. As its darkness closes in over them, they almost refuse to believe that God is love. Many pass through it and come out of it without receiving any divine comfort. They did not know why they were there. They did not wait silently to receive the teaching and the blessing of Jesus. Others, who entered trembling, can testify that it was the death of a little one that first led them truly to know Jesus. As truly as to Jairus with his dead daughter, the child's death was the parent's life.

Alone With God

Let us see how Jesus meets the needs of the

sorrowing parents. The first thing He asks is silence and solitude. Jesus comes to the house and finds the crowd making a great commotion. At once He puts out the crowd and goes in alone, with the parents and the three disciples. One of the things that hinders the blessing of affliction is that too much time is spent conversing with people and seeking comfort in their sympathy. One of God's objectives is to draw the soul to Himself. We must have an attitude of silent meditation while waiting to hear the voice of God. He has lessons, often difficult lessons, to teach the parents whose little one has been taken away by death. When there is a teachable spirit that really looks to God and waits on Him, the trail becomes fruitful in blessing.

The parent is led to ask, Have I loved my child in the Lord or looked upon him too much as my own possession? Has the spirit of my life and my home been to educate my children for heaven and its holiness? Has worldliness, selfishness, or sinfulness gotten in the way of my parental duties? Affliction can never profit without heart searching. Heart searching requires the holy stillness of soul that is found in separation from man and meeting with God.

Let parents beware, in their time of trial, of the distractions that come from seeing too many friends, from seeking and finding comfort in their company. God wants to see us alone. Without solitude He cannot bless or comfort us. Jesus waits to reveal Himself in the power of His great salvation—the Redeemer in whom the parent will find all the grace and blessing God has promised. Jesus cannot do this unless the crowd is put outside. He takes His three disciples with Him to remind us that, by the bedside of a dying or a dead child, Jesus wants to be alone with the parents. Even His ministers are only to come in as they come with Him and to Him.

Jesus Brings Comfort

When He is alone with the parents, Jesus speaks the comforting words, "Weep not." Jesus does not condemn weeping. He wept Himself; weeping always touched His heart. And yet He says, "Weep not." "Woman, why weepest thou?" was His very first resurrection word (see John 20:13). Jesus came to dry our tears. He says, "Weep not." Weeping is often a self-indulgent nursing of our grief. It is the fruit of being too absorbed in ourselves, the person who died, or the suffering we endure.

Weeping often hinders the voice of God being heard, and hinders the blessing the affliction was meant to bring. We are occupied with how we are suffering, but God would have us think of the cause of the suffering and the sin which made Him suffer. God wants to take us away from ourselves to make room in our hearts for Himself. Weeping often only fills us with ourselves. God would have us learn in the affliction to love and worship His will. Weeping is often the adoration of our own will.

Beloved mourner, hear the voice of Jesus say,

"Weep not." He does not say it without a reason. It is not enough that the commotion of the crowd is put outside and that there is silence in the room. The thoughts and feelings of the grieving parents must be silenced. At the request of Jesus the tears must be restrained, and our heart must turn to Him. Obedience to this command is the path to the comfort He brings.

What is the comfort Jesus gives? He leads from the visible to the invisible. Where we see only death, He speaks of life. He comes to rouse us to faith and to reveal Himself as the living and life-giving One. "Weep not: she is not dead, but sleepeth." With these words Jesus draws near to the lifeless form of each little one over whom a mother's bursting heart is weeping. He reminds her that death has been conquered, and the loved one is not dead in the terrible meaning which sin gave that word.

Your little one is not dead. Judge not by sight. There is a better life than the life of this earth—the eternal life in which God dwells. Eternal life and the glory in which it shall be fully manifested is something that has not entered the human heart. In the same way, this sleep is something that passes knowledge. We only know for certain that it is a most blessed rest, rest in the bosom of Jesus. We are comforted to know that our little one, whom Jesus took into His covenant, is now resting with Him.

Coming To Know Jesus

It is Jesus, Himself, who comes to the parent to speak these things. In the Old Testament it was the God of the covenant who came to believing parents with His promise of what their children should be. In the New Testament it is Jesus, the Surety of the children, in whom the parent will find the grace for all he needs to train his child for God. Jesus said, "Believe Me that I am in the Father, and the Father in Me. . .he that hath seen Me hath seen the Father" (John 14:11,9). In the incarnation of Jesus, all that God had promised of blessing to parents and children is now fulfilled. If we learn to know Jesus, to believe on Him fully and to live by faith in Him, our home and family life will be holy to the Lord. No sacrifice is too great if we only learn to know Jesus better. It was in the chamber where Jairus' daughter lay dead that her parents learned to know Jesus.

Weeping parents, this is God's one purpose and desire, this is God's one great thought of blessing and comfort: in His Son, Christ Jesus, He has come near to bless and take possession of you. Let this, your time of affliction, not pass without experiencing Jesus as the parents' friend, teacher, comforter, and sanctifier. The loss you have sustained will be restored tenfold in the blessing it is made to yourself and the children still left you. Or even if he were the only child, this new knowledge of Jesus will enable you to bring blessing to others. The presence, power, and love of Jesus can more than compensate for the absence and loss of the child.

A Parent's Prayer

Blessed Lord, in this my hour of deep sorrow, I come to You, my Savior and the Savior of my little one. Come in with me, my Lord, and be my comforter and my teacher. Put out the tumult of the crowd, the sad thoughts, and uncontrolled feelings that keep me from hearing Your voice. Speak to the storm, Be still! And let Your presence be the great calm.

Speak, Lord, and comfort Your child. Reveal Yourself to me as the resurrection and the life, the shepherd who has taken His lamb into His bosom. Reveal Yourself as my shepherd, by coming nearer to me with Your abiding presence. Reveal Yourself as the family friend, making Yourself at home with us. Amen.

Chapter 38

THE WIDOW AND HER CHILDREN

"There was a dead man carried out, the only son of his mother, and she was a widow. . .and when the Lord saw her, He had compassion on her, and said unto her, Weep not"—Luke 7:12,13.

Any attempt to present the teachings of Scripture concerning the raising of children would certainly be incomplete if it had nothing to say about a woman raising her children alone. It is one of the most difficult trials that can happen to a woman. The husband on whom she had counted as her guide, in whom her life and her love found their joy, to whom she looked as her help and strength in the raising of her children, is taken from her. She is left alone and desolate. The sight of her children, instead of being a treasure to which her love now clings, only adds new bitterness to her situation.

God's Concern For Widows

It is not only the human heart that is saddened

by the widow's grief, the heart of God is also touched. From the repeated command in the law of Moses down to James's testimony, Scripture teaches us "to visit the fatherless and widows in their affliction" (James 1:27). God never forgets the widow. "A Father of the fatherless, and a Judge of the widows, is God in His holy habitation" (Psalm 68:5). "He relieveth the fatherless and the widow" (Psalm 146:9). "Leave thy fatherless children, I will preserve them alive; and let thy widows trust in me" (Jeremiah 49:11). Such words reveal to us the very heart of God.

When Jesus came, how could He fail to show in this, too, that He was the Father's image, that God was in Christ. It is as if the picture of the Master's life would be incomplete without the story of the widow of Nain. Here, we see Him as the comforter of widowed motherhood. Let us go to Nain, the sacred spot to which so many a widow has resorted in order to find Jesus, her friend. Let us learn what Jesus has to say to a widow weeping over her child. When the tears are those of sorrow over one taken away, or tears of anxious love at the sight of those still left behind, Jesus still meets us with His, "Weep not."

Weep not, widowed mother, as you look at your little ones, and your heart almost breaks at the thought of their being fatherless. Weep not, but come, follow me, as we seek Him who has been anointed "to comfort all that mourn" (Isaiah 61:2). Weep not, as you tremble to think of how you are to raise and educate your children all alone. Let your soul for a little while be silent unto Him who came from heaven to say to the widow, "As one whom his mother comforteth, so will I comfort you" (Isaiah 66:13).

Jesus Comforts The Widow

Weep not! Can the wounded heart, at least, have the comfort that the unrestrained flow of its tears often brings? Just think for a little moment. The widow of Nain did not know why Jesus spoke to her this way. Let it be enough that Jesus says it. All the other parents whose children Jesus blessed came and asked for help, but He speaks to the widow without being asked. Her widowhood is her sufficient plea: "When the Lord saw her, He had compassion on her, and said unto her, Weep not." Jesus is looking on you; do not let your tears keep you from looking and listening to Him. If it could have been, He would have spared you this trial. Now that it has come, He is looking on you in compassion, waiting to comfort and to bless you. In the tenderest love, but with the voice of authority Jesus says, Weep not.

Jesus did not comfort only with words—His words were always followed by deeds. If you will look up and see, He will show you what He will do. To the widowed mother at Nain, He gave back the dead son who had helped take the place of her husband. His believing people know that the departed ones who have died in the Lord will be given back to them in glory forever. Look up to Jesus, the Resurrection and the Life, weeping widow, and believe. The resurrection, the meeting again, the being ever with the Lord, are realities, more real, more mighty than the separation and the sorrow. Look up in faith, it is Jesus who speaks, "Weep not."

But oh, the desolation that fills the heart. What a sense of utter weakness the widow feels! The responsibility of raising her children seems too great. The boys and girls, who still live, need a father's wise, firm, loving rule. Dear mother, when Jesus says, "Weep not," He never speaks without doing. He gives what can dry the tears. If Jesus were to take the place of the father for these children, you would smile and sing even through the tears. If, as a living reality, Jesus would undertake the responsibility of educating your children, of being your adviser, your strength, and your assurance of success in your work, would this be enough to keep back those tears? And this is just what He comes to do. God spoke in the Old Testament, "Leave thy fatherless children. . .and let thy widows trust in Me;" and "The Lord relieveth the fatherless and the widow." Jesus comes in human tenderness, in the nearness of the Holy Spirit, to fulfill these words. You may trust your fatherless children to Him. He will preserve them. He will, in divine power, be the Father of the fatherless.

Trust In Jesus

It may be that a widowed mother reads these words, but they have little meaning. Though a Christian, she has not learned to live by faith. She

237

has not learned to consider the unseen things of faith surer and clearer than the things of sight. To her the promise appears vague and distant. She hardly dares hope that Jesus will be to her all He has promised. She feels she is not worthy enough for her children to receive such special and divine guidance.

My sister, you may with confidence depend upon your children being preserved and blessed by Jesus. Let your tears pass away in the sunlight of His love and care, as you come and listen. Of a widow He asks but one thing—"Let thy widows *trust in Me.*" "She that is a widow *trusteth in God,* and continueth in supplication and prayer night and day" (see Jeremiah 49:11 and 1 Timothy 5:5). This was what He claimed from the widow of Nain; this is what He asks of you. *Trust Jesus!* This is the message I bring you this day in your weeping, anxious widowhood. Trust Him for yourself. Let each thought of your departed loved one lead you to say, I have Jesus with me—I will trust Him. Let your awareness of sin and your shortcomings awaken the prayer within you, "Jesus! I will trust You to make me what I should be."

Trust Him with your children, with their temporal and their eternal needs. Only remember the life of trust requires a life of undivided, simple, childlike surrender. In prayer and supplication, commit every care and fear to Him. Really trust Him and in every prayer make this your main confession: I have now entrusted my need to Him, I trust Him with it. I am confident, He is mighty and faithful to keep that which I have committed unto Him. Trust Him completely. You will find Him completely true.

If the double trial of the widow of Nain should ever be yours, and you have to mourn the loss of a husband and a son, remember that Jesus is still the comforter of the widow. This will be the time you will find Him doubly precious. You will have grace to say, My flesh and my heart fail; but God, but Jesus, is the strength of my heart, and my portion forever.

A Parent's Prayer

Savior, strengthen the faith of every widow. Let her sorrow and her weakness compel her to cast herself with her children on You, to depend upon You alone. Draw Yourself near and reveal Yourself to her. Speak to her sorrowing, anxious heart Your word of comfort: Weep not! Oh, let her hear You speaking, see You come to take charge, and provide for the raising of her children. Teach her that her one work is to trust You, in separation from the world, in holy devotedness to You, to trust You for divine guidance and blessing on her children. Let her continue to pray in daily communion with You, the Father of her children. Let her know how truly You are the widow's friend, the child's friend, and the Savior of both widow and child. Amen.

Chapter 39

WHEN YOUR CHILD IS SICK

"There was a certain nobleman, whose son was sick at Capernaum. . . .He went unto (Jesus), and besought Him that He would come down, and heal his son; for he was at the point of death"—John 4:46,47.

Here is an experience that almost every parent passes through. In the parent's relationship with his child, the sickroom is often the place where the parent is able to lead the child to Jesus. The beautiful story of the nobleman of Capernaum teaches us how sickness is to be met, healed, and used by God.

Meet Sickness With Faith

How is sickness to be met? God's great gift to sinful men is Jesus. In His Son, He meets our every need. The one great thing God asks of us is to have faith—the trustful surrender to let Jesus be to us all that the Father would have Him be. Faith has been given to us as parents for us to use on behalf of our children, until we can lead them to accept

Him for themselves.

Faith in God was the one thing by which the saints of old pleased God and did all that was pleasing to Him. In the same way, faith in His Son is the one supreme grace by which the Christian parent can please God and obtain His blessings on his children. All God's leadings and dealings have this one object and purpose—to make us strong in faith, giving glory to God.

When sickness comes upon a young child, the parents' hearts are agonized by the sight of his pain or the fear of losing the child. Then the question comes with terrible force, Why does God permit all this suffering? God's one purpose with parent and child is to work and increase faith in them. By faith they become capable of receiving the revelation of God's glory. By faith God can dwell in them and work through them. God's one desire is that they should believe more fully in His Son. Our one desire should be to meet the sickness by faith in Jesus.

This is the one great lesson the story of the nobleman teaches us—the growth and increase of faith in Christ. The nobleman's faith begins as a general faith in what he has heard of Christ's compassion and power. This brings him into contact with Christ. He believes in Jesus as a healer. It becomes a distinct faith in the promise he received of healing: "the man believed the word that Jesus had spoken unto him" (John 4:50). He believes in Jesus as the Healer of his child. Then the faith in Jesus, the healer, is perfected in the faith in Him as Savior and Lord: "himself believed, and his whole house" (verse 53).

Claim Your Child's Healing

How is the sickness to be healed? This is the second question our story suggests. The answer it gives is very simple: by the power of Jesus. In Matthew, Christ's healing work is spoken of as the natural result of His atoning work of which Isaiah had spoken. (See Isaiah 53:5 and Matthew 8:17.) When on earth, Jesus delighted in healing the sick as something His loving heart could do for them even when He could not save their souls. In His Word, He left the assurance that the prayer of faith would save the sick, because the prayer of a righteous man availeth much.

Jesus expects us to apply the promise of an answer to believing prayer and thus to believe and receive the healing of a sick child. His great desire in sickness is to teach us that simple, childlike faith brings the assurance that our petition is granted. We have what we ask. Let us claim the life of the beloved sick one for God's glory in him and in us as parents. The word of Jesus can come to us as real as to the nobleman: thy son liveth.

Draw Near To Jesus

Sickness can be used to draw people to Jesus. When it has done this, Jesus takes it away, so that the healing binds them to Himself. Healing perfects what sickness begins. The sickness brought the nobleman to Jesus in hope and expectancy.

The healing left him a confirmed believer, along with his household.

Some people believe that sickness is better than health in accomplishing true holiness. In the life and work of Christ, we see no evidence of this idea. Health obtained directly from Jesus in the prayer of faith, as a gift of redeeming love, is one of the most wonderful spiritual blessings. Health reveals the hand of Jesus in the body. Let each parent realize that health received in faith brings much greater blessing than sickness or even healing. Once we understand this, we will have courage to make known our desire for health for God's glory. This new revelation of the power and the love of Jesus may make us, and our household, believers as never before—full of faith and devotion to Him who has blessed us.

Sickness calls us to search our heart, life, and home as to whether we have kept our children completely for God and trained them as holy to the Lord. It makes the heart tender and humble and draws us to Jesus. God wants to bring us, subdued and quiet, in faith and hope to Jesus. Our exercise of faith honors God more than anything. The trusting of Jesus' word and power, the learning to know Him as our Helper, the experience of His healing power in distinct answer to our faith—it is this that binds us to Christ. We learn to know Him as the living One. Our home becomes a place to display His kingly power.

A Parent's Prayer

Lord Jesus, teach us during the time of our children's sickness to learn the blessed lesson of coming to You and trusting You. We can be sure that You are watching over us to teach, to comfort, to sanctify, and to heal. Teach us especially that You are still the same as when you were on earth—mighty to command the sickness to depart and to free from the power of death. You are still ready to hear the prayer of faith and raise up the child. Oh, grant us this faith, that we may honor You and not hinder You from proving with what compassion You hear a parent's cry. Lord, when You have graciously heard and given back a child to the parent's faith, grant that the parents with their whole house believe in You as never before. May all see that Jesus is now Lord and Master, the beloved Friend of the home. As sickness leads us to seek You, may Your healing bind us to You and Your blessed service. Amen.

Chapter 40

FEED MY LAMBS

"Jesus saith to Simon Peter. . .Lovest thou me more than these? He saith unto him, Yea, Lord; thou knowest that I love thee. He saith unto him, Feed my lambs"—John 21:15.

Peter was a fisherman. After the first miraculous draught of fishes, the Lord had said, "Follow Me, and I will make you fishers of men" (Matthew 4:19). Peter's work on earth was made the symbol of his heavenly calling. After the resurrection when Jesus appeared on the shore, he no longer calls Peter a fisherman, but a shepherd. There is a deep meaning in the change. There is one great point of difference between the fisherman and the shepherd. The fisherman catches what he has neither reared nor fed. He seeks only what is full-grown, casting away all the little fish out of his net back into the sea. The shepherd directs his special attention to the young and the weak. All the shepherd's profit depends on how he cares for the lambs.

The example of the fisherman provided no way

for the Master to give special instructions concerning the children of His Church. The shepherd's calling at once suggested the words, "Feed My lambs," and presents the deep importance and the blessed reward of giving first place to the little ones of the flock. Peter, and all Christ's ministers, were not only to feed the sheep, but the prosperity of the Church would especially depend upon their feeding the lambs. What was said to them is especially applicable to parents as under-shepherds who each have their little flock of lambs to keep and raise for the Master. Christ's commission to His Church through Peter shows the place the little ones have in His heart. It teaches us to think of the weakness, the value, the need, and the hope of our children.

The Weakness Of Children

"Feed My *lambs*," Jesus says, and reminds us of the frailty of our children and their spiritual life. I was once leaving a sheep farm after having visited with the owner. Toward evening there were threatening clouds. He hurried back, crying out to his son, "Take great care of the lambs! There is a storm coming!"

The Lord Jesus was just about to ascend to heaven when He gave one of His last words: "Care for the lambs." The sheep is a weak and helpless animal—how much more helpless is the little lamb! It cannot care for itself. The Master wants every minister and every parent to think how dependent the child is on the care of those to whom he is entrusted. The child cannot choose the company under whose influence he comes. He does not yet know to choose between good and evil. The child knows nothing of the importance of little words or deeds, of forming habits, of sowing good or bad seed, of yielding himself to the world or God. All depends upon his surroundings. Parents especially have the children in their power. What a solemn responsibility to lead and nourish them carefully, to feed them with food which our Father has provided, to lead them only in the green pastures!

The High Value Of Children

Feed *My* lambs: these words remind us of the high value of the little ones. In the lambs, the shepherd sees the possibilities of the future: the lambs are the coming flock. The Church of the next generation, the servants whom Jesus will use to do His work of converting and saving and blessing men, are the children of today. How little we have understood or heeded the voice—feed the lambs.

He also says, "Feed *My* lambs, for of such is the kingdom." Jesus loves children not only for what they are to become, but for what they already are in their childlike simplicity and heavenliness. He considers them of great worth for the lessons they continually have to teach grown-up people and the influence they exert in making their parents and elders gentle, humble, and trustful. They bring many blessings to those who receive them in the name of Jesus. They are to Him of unspeakable worth, the most beautiful part of His flock.

Let us try to catch His spirit as He cries, "Feed *My* lambs." Oh, let us learn to look upon our children in the light in which Jesus looks upon them! Let us pray for the Holy Spirit to make the familiar words, Jesus' lambs, a deep spiritual reality to us, until our hearts tremble at the thought. Our little ones are His lambs: we are to feed them daily that they may grow up as the sheep of His pasture.

The Needs Of Children

Feed My lambs: the children's great need is presented to us. Food is the condition of growth. Food is something received from without, to be assimilated and taken into our very life. The body has its food from the visible world. The mind is nourished by the thoughts that enter it. The spirit feeds, through the mind, on the thoughts, the words of God. The little ones cannot seek pasture for themselves. Christ looks to parents to bring to them divine wisdom and love, without which the soul cannot possibly grow.

In the same way that the mother plans daily what the child is to eat, she must spiritually feed each lamb entrusted to her care. Her one desire and aim must be to raise the child for Him. The consecration of the child to the Lord must be the chief thing in his life. The idea that the child is the Lord's and he is growing up entirely and alone for Him will make the duty easy.

The Test Of Love

Feed my lambs: the words tell the provision Christ has made for His little ones. To whom were the words spoken? To one of whom the question had been asked, "Lovest thou Me?" and who had answered, "Yea, Lord, Thou knowest that I love Thee." It is only one who is inspired by love for Jesus who can truly take charge of the lambs. This is the test to determine whether the parent is qualified to be a shepherd of the lambs—"Lovest thou Me?" This is the provision Jesus has made for the lambs: true love to Jesus can do the work.

Let every parent who longs to know how he can obtain the needed qualification for his work submit his name for this test. Let Jesus search your heart—once, twice, a third time—until the remembrance of your past unfaithfulness brings tears; and the answer comes, "Lord, You know all things, You know that I do love You." It is this that is the problem in so many a Christian home— the conscious, fervent, and confessed love of Jesus is lacking. Nothing influences a child like love: the warmth of a holy love for Jesus will make itself felt. There may be a great deal of religion, teaching, and praying; but only love will conquer.

Love for Jesus will lead the parent to obey Him very carefully, to walk with Him very closely, to trust Him very heartily. Love for Jesus will make the desire to please Him very strong, and the duty He gives us very precious. Love for Jesus will make our testimony of Him very personal. The food with which we feed the lambs will have the warmth of a divine love about it. Jesus needs parents who love Him, who love Him with their whole heart and strength: this is the provision He has made for His little lambs.

The Special Love Of Parents

The religion of Jesus is a religion of love. Of the Father it is said, "God is love" (1 John 4:8). Jesus Himself is the gift of love that passes knowledge. His own life and work is one of love—love stronger than death. When the Holy Spirit comes to us, He sheds abroad in our hearts the love of God. Our whole relationship to the divine is to be one of love. Our relationship as parents and children was meant to be one of love. It was to restore this that Jesus came. He does it by calling parents to love Him and to receive the little ones in His name. He purifies and elevates the love of earth by the love of heaven. The home is consecrated by the light of Jesus' love resting on the children, the power of His love dwelling in the parents, and the raising of children being made a work of love for Him.

Christian parents, see and accept your blessed calling. You are the shepherds of the divine love to tend and feed the lambs. In His Church the Chief Shepherd has many shepherds to care for the flock, but none who can care for the lambs as parents do. "He maketh Him families like a flock" (Psalm 107:41). It is to parental love, inspired and sanctified by redeeming love, that Jesus looks for the building of His Church.

Let us pray very earnestly to have our eyes
opened to see things as Jesus sees them. May we
realize by the Holy Spirit what He feels for our
little ones. May we know what He expects of us
and is ready to do for us in giving us wisdom and
strength. Feed My lambs: when this word is made
the law of a parent's duty, what gentleness and
love it will inspire. The result will be: heavenly
hope; faithful, watchful care; and an unceasing
life of faith in the love and blessing of Jesus on our
home! Let us often wait for the voice to say to us,
"Lovest thou Me? Feed My lambs."

A Parent's Prayer

Blessed Savior, You are the good shepherd of
whom my soul has said, "The Lord is *my* Shepherd, I shall not want." Thank You for the holy
privilege of being a parent and fulfilling Your
commission: "Feed My lambs." My Lord, may my
daily experience of Your shepherd love teach me
how to feed my little flocks of lambs. Blessed
Master, I ask You to open my eyes to look upon my
children as You do, to regard them in the light of
Your claim upon them. To this end, my Lord, fill
me with Your love. I confess with shame that there
has been in my life so little of an enthusiastic love
for You. Lord, forgive me and deliver me. Let obedient love for you be the atmosphere of the home
in which my children grow up. O Lamb of God,
who allows my children to be God's lambs, let
Your holy love in my heart inspire my relationship

251

with You and with them. Let me prove how wonderfully You are my shepherd and how blessedly I am their shepherd. Amen.

Chapter 41

THE HOLY SPIRIT IN THE FAMILY

"The promise is unto you, and to your children"—Acts 2:39.

We have not forgotten the frequent use in the Old Testament of the words in which parents and children were joined together as partners in God's covenant and blessings. "Thou *and* thy house," "Thee *and* thy seed," "You *and* your children," "Me *and* my house," such were the expressions of the blessed bond that made the whole family one in God's sight. The expression is found in the New Testament, too. "You and your children." Nowhere could it have found a place of deeper significance than in the second chapter of Acts. On the day of Pentecost, as the Church of Christ receives its baptism of the Holy Spirit, the word is heard, "The promise is unto you, *and* to your children." All the blessings of the new ministry of the Spirit are at once secured for our children.

The Promise Given To Your Children

"The promise is unto you, and to *your chil-*

dren." The promise is of the Spirit of the glorified Jesus, in all His fullness, the baptism of fire and of power. When we are baptized in the name of the Father, and of the Son, and of the Holy Spirit, we confess our faith in the Holy Trinity. We confess our faith in the Holy Spirit, not only as one with the Father and the Son, but as being the third person, who brings the perfect revelation of the divine glory. All that God promised in the Old Covenant is now made our very own by the Holy Spirit. Through Him all the promises of God are fulfilled, all grace and salvation in Christ become a personal possession and experience. God's Word calls our children children of promise. It is especially this promise of the Holy Spirit that they are the heirs of.

The secret of godly child-rearing is to bring them up in the *faith* and for the *fulfillment* of this promise. In the *faith of the promise* we must learn to look upon the presence of the Spirit in our daily training as absolutely necessary, but also as most positively given to us. In our prayers, in our family devotions and daily life, we must learn to expect the direct working of the Holy Spirit. In this way we will train our children for the *fulfillment of the promise*. Then, from childhood to adult life, their lives will be holy to the Lord.

The Promise Given To You

The promise is unto *you* and your children. The very thought of training children to be dependent upon the Holy Spirit's presence appears strange and impractical to some people. The reason for their thinking this way is simply that they have not yet learned to understand and enjoy the abiding of the Spirit as essential to a true Christian life. The promise of the Spirit is to *you*. Parents must realize in their own personal experience that it is only the continual leading of the Spirit that enables us to live as God would have us. Then they will have the capacity for believing the promise of the Spirit for their children. Only in this way can they become the ministers of the Spirit to their families.

The source of all complaints about the failure of religious education in the Church is that the Holy Spirit is not accepted as the only sufficient strength of the believer. Will *you* parents, who have received the promise, receive it for your children, too?

The Unity Of Parent And Child

The promise is unto you *and* your children. As in nature, so in grace, you *and* your children have been linked together for good or for evil. Physically, intellectually, morally, they are the partakers of your life. Spiritually this can also be true. The gift of the Spirit and His gracious workings, to you and to them, does not consist of two distinct separate acts. Rather, the Spirit comes in and through you. Your life, your daily influence, is the channel through which His quickening and sanctifying grace can reach them.

If you are resting content with the thought that

255

you are saved, without seeking to be truly filled with the Spirit—if your life is still more carnal than spiritual, with more of the spirit of the world than of God—do not think it is strange if your children grow up unconverted. This is only right and natural. You are hindering the Holy Spirit. You are breathing day by day into your children the spirit of the world. You are using all your influence to train them in man's religion, in harmony with the spirit of the world, instead of God's religion, in the power of the Holy Spirit sent down from heaven. The promise is to you *and* to your children. In spite of your evil influence, the blessing may reach them through the faith of others. However, you have no reason to expect it, except as you yield yourselves to be the channel for its conveyance. May our parental love lead us to see that, for our children's sake, nothing less is needed than for us to be filled with the Holy Spirit.

The Promise Of The Holy Spirit

The promise is unto you and your children. *The promise!* All parents should understand what is implied in the promise. Too many look upon a promise of God as a mere word or thought—something that is without power until they do what is necessary to make it effectual. They do not know that the Word of God has in it a living, mighty energy, a divine seed-life. If they will but hide and keep it in their hearts, it will produce the faith through which the blessed fulfillment comes.

256

The promise of the Holy Spirit, in His fullness and His power, is to you and to your children. A promise means that God, in His infinite power, has bound Himself to do what He has said. He will most certainly do it for us as soon as we claim it in faith. The promise here means that the Holy Spirit is ours, waiting to come and be in our home all that we need to make it holy and happy. Our home life may yet be far from God's ideal. It may appear impossible to us in our circumstances and with our difficulties that we will ever succeed in making it very different. However, if we will but claim and hold fast the promise in the prayer of faith, God Himself will fulfill it.

A promise needs two things: the receiver must believe and claim it; the giver must fulfill it and make it true. Let our attitude be that of simple, trustful faith in God for ourselves and our children, counting on the promise: God is faithful, who will also do it.

Dear fellow-parents, let us humble ourselves because we have not proved the truth and the glory of this promise. Let us confess with shame how much there has been that was carnal and not spiritual—of the spirit of the world, and not of the Spirit of God in our lives. Let us open our hearts to take in the promise of God as something that has a divine quickening power. It is something that will produce in us the very state of mind which God requires before the fulfillment comes. Let us look upon ourselves as the divinely-appointed ministers of the Holy Spirit, to prepare and train our children under His influence from their youth up. Let us yield ourselves completely to His guidance and working. To properly train a child means training him to be a temple of the Holy Spirit. To do that we, ourselves, must be living in the power of the Spirit.

Let us place our lives as parents under the leading of the Holy Spirit. That will mean placing our entire life under His leading. We can be to our children only what we really are to God. Let us thank God for giving us the grace to make our family life the sphere for the special working of His Spirit. Let it be our unceasing prayer and our confident expectation that, by the power of the Holy Spirit, our home on earth will become more like the home in heaven.

A Parent's Prayer

O God, we open the doors of our beloved home to You and place our family life under the rule of Your Holy Spirit. We ask You to take possession of it. As parents we desire to claim the fulfillment of the promise. May the invisible atmosphere that surrounds us and that fills our home be that which Your Holy Spirit breathes—one of holiness to the Lord. We claim the promise for our children. We desire, in simple, childlike faith, to consider it as a settled thing between You and us; they are the heirs of the promise of the Spirit. Our Father, we want to guide our home life and train each child day by day under the leading of the Holy Spirit. Amen.

Chapter 42

THE PARENT'S EXAMPLE

"Thou therefore which teachest another, teachest thou not thyself?" —Romans 2:21.

Nothing can be more inconsistent and vain than the attempt to teach others without teaching ourselves. Only the lessons which the teacher really masters and has thoroughly made his own can be successfully communicated to others. In the same way, it is only the lesson I first teach myself that I can really teach my child. One of the first laws in the science of child raising is that it depends far more on example than explanation. *What parents are means more than what they say*. All the great lessons of childhood, the parent must first learn himself. Let us look at some of them.

The Parent's Example Of Self-Control

The great aim of education is to give the child, when grown to manhood, the perfect mastery and the ready use of all the talents and abilities God has given him. To this end, self-control is one of the most important virtues. A country cannot prosper if there is no wise, intelligent ruler to make its laws and provide for its needs as they arise. In the same way there can be no happiness in the little empire within man's heart unless everything is subject to a ruling power. The child must be trained early in habits of quiet thoughtfulness of speech and action, giving time and opportunity for their mind and will to rule.

This training comes far more through example then precept. It is the atmosphere of a well-regulated home, and the influence of the parents' self-control, which leaves its mark on the child. When parents act with impulse and temper, the effect of their good advice is more than neutralized by the evil influence of the spirit they displayed. It is the spirit that influences. God's Word says, "Thou therefore which teacheth another, teachest thou not thyself?" If parents honestly watch themselves, they will often discover the causes for their children's shortcomings. Such discovery ought to lead parents to very earnest confession before God, to a hearty surrender to the teaching of Jesus and the Holy Spirit. We can depend upon divine renewal to equip us for true self-control. What we, by grace, teach ourselves will in due time influence our children, too.

The Parent's Example Of Obedience

Self-control must know its objective and the path used to reach that objective. The child finds both in the word we have already repeated so often—obedience. He must control himself to be able to render obedience to his parents, so that he may be trained to obey God. Here again the parent's obedience will be contagious, it will inspire the child.

"Johnny," said a father once to a child, who was hesitating about obeying his father's will, "whose will must you do, your own or papa's?" "Papa's will," was the reluctant answer. But the child immediately asked, "But whose will must Papa do, then?" The father was able at once to answer, "God's will." He could explain how he considered obedience to a wiser and better will than his own his greatest privilege. He could at once take his place by the side of his child as also having to give up his own will.

The parent whose children know that he seeks to do the will of his God in all things will be able to instill obedience in the child. When, on the contrary, the seeking of our own will characterizes our relationship with our children, we need not wonder why their training is a failure. Let us turn at once and listen to the voice, "Thou that teachest another, teachest thou not thyself?"

The Parent's Example Of Love

Family life has been ordained of God as the place where love can be cultivated. Our self-control is proved by the way we love others and restrain everything that is selfish or unloving. In the daily life of our children, we have in miniature the temptations to which later life will expose them. There will be ample opportunities for them to exercise the virtues of gentleness and patience, forgiveness and generostiy, helpfulness and love. Principles must not only be instilled, but the trouble must be taken to lead the child to do the right thing easily and lovingly.

Many people wish to help the poor, for instance, but they do not do anything because they do not know how to go about it. One of the highest goals of Christian education is to make deeds of kindness the chief aim in life. Our desire should be to live to make those around us better and happier. This can only be attained as the parents teach themselves and cultivate the virtues they seek to instill in their children.

In the daily life of the family, the parents must seek to prove that love is the law of their life. It must be understood that unkind words, harsh judgments, and unloving reports are not part of their conversation. In the parents' relationship with each other, with their children, with friends, and the world around, love, God's love, must be sought after and manifested. The example of Christ and His love must be reduced to practice in daily life. Only then can the parent's training of their children to love be fully successful.

The Parent's Role As A Student

"Thou that teachest another, teachest thou not thyself?" These words ask whether as parents we are doing the first and most important thing for being successful teachers of our children: teaching ourselves. Yes, parents, teach yourselves. If we are to train our children wisely, we must go through a new course of training ourselves. We have to put ourselves in school again and be teachers and students at the same time.

All schooling requires time and trouble, patience and payment. Teaching that costs nothing is of little value. No one can graduate as even fairly competent to train a child for eternity, without making sacrifices. Take time to study God's Word and what it says of a parent's duties. Study man's moral nature, with its wonderful capacities, as the sacred trust committed to your care. Teach yourself to cultivate that nature to its highest ability for God's service: it will be the best preparation for teaching your children.

If you feel how much you need the help of some friend to stimulate and to guide—let Jesus be that teacher. He came and taught Himself, that He might know how to teach us to obey. He learned obedience that He might show us the way to the Father and reveal the Father's love and grace. He will not refuse to teach and enable us to be true fathers and mothers to our children. We will understand that to be teachable, obedient, loving children of the Heavenly Father is the surest way of having our children teachable, obedient, and loving, too.

A Parent's Prayer

Gracious God, I come again to seek the grace I need for fulfilling my role as a parent. I ask of You to imprint deep on my heart the solemn thought that I can effectually teach my children only what I really teach myself. I can only expect the truth that influences my own life to influence theirs.

Lord God, I think with shame how much of my children's behavior is only the reflection of what they have seen in me. I confess how much there has been lacking of that spirit of childlike love, of joyful obedience to You, and self-sacrifice for others. My example should have been to them a form of the highest education. O my God, forgive me for what is past. Give me grace in everything to teach myself what I want to teach my children. Amen.

Chapter 43

HOLY PARENTS—HOLY CHILDREN

"Now are (your children) holy"—1 Corinthians 7:14.

Let us praise God for this precious sentence. There is not a deeper or more distinctly divine word in Scripture than holy. In this statement the whole treasure of holiness, with all that revelation teaches us concerning it, is made the heritage of our children. God's holiness and our children are meant for each other. As parents we are the God-ordained links for bringing them into perfect union. If we are to do this, we must understand and apply this precious truth. The revelation of God's holiness was a very gradual one, because it was the opening up of the mystery of the Holy Trinity. There was first holiness as seen in God, its source and fountain; then in Christ, the Holy One of God, our sanctification; then in the Holy Spirit, as the Spirit of holiness in the Church. It is only by gradual steps that we can rise from the lower to the higher use of the word and enter into the fullness of divine meaning which the word has used

of our children.

A Holy Relationship

The word *holy* expresses a relationship. Whatever was separated unto God and made His property was called holy. "The Lord will shew who are His and who is holy. . .the man whom the Lord doth choose, he shall be holy" (Numbers 16:5,7). Whatever had been given to God and taken by Him to be His own was holy.

So the first and simplest thought our faith must take in and fill with spiritual meaning is this: our children belong to God. The very fact of their being born to believing parents make them His in a very special sense. In Bible times the children of the slaves were the property of the master as much as the slave himself. Also, the Lord's redeemed, who love to call themselves His bond-servants, look upon their children in the same way they see themselves—absolutely His. "Now are your children holy."

A Destiny And A Power

The word *holy* suggests a destiny. It is of great importance, as we study the word holy in Scripture, to notice how everything that is called holy had a use and purpose. Every holy day and thing, place and person had its service to fulfill. Let the Christian parent beware of looking upon holiness as a mere means to an end, simply as the way to safely get to heaven. Oh, it is infinitely more! Let him consent that his child is God's property, to be used in this world only as God directs, to be trained with the one purpose of doing God's will, and to show forth God's glory. The more clearly this is understood and made the distinct object of the work of prayer and education, the more speedily we will grasp what the word *holy* contains in its higher meaning.

The word *holy* is the promise of a divine life-power. Let us beware of emptying the word *holy* of its divine truth and power. If God calls our children holy, it is because they are born from a believing parent who is holy in Christ; therefore, they are holy, too. The child of true believers inherits from his parents, not only the sinful nature, but habits and tendencies which the child of the unbeliever does not share. These are the true seeds of holiness, the working of the Holy Spirit from the mother's womb. Even where it cannot be seen, there is a secret heritage of the seed of holiness implanted in the child of the believer. There is secured to him the Holy Spirit in whom the holiness of God has reached its full manifestation.

In promising the Holy Spirit to His disciples, our Lord said He would be a river of living water flowing from them to others. The believer has power to influence those with whom he comes in contact. The child born of him inherits a blessing in the very life he receives from the parent who is sanctified by the indwelling of the Holy Spirit. In the mother's womb the child can receive the Holy Spirit. Oh, let us be sure of it, when God gives our child the name *holy,* that is the beginning of the work of His own Holy Spirit. Let nothing less than this be what our heart reads in God's words: your children are holy.

God's Character

The word holy describes a character. God's holiness is His infinite moral perfection. He hates and destroys evil. He loves and uses good. Holiness is the divine energy of which perfect righteousness and infinite love are the revelation. It is unity with Himself that God seeks and gives. "Be ye holy; I am holy; I make holy." In calling your children *holy,* God invites you to have them partakers of *His* holiness; without this, holiness is but a name and a shadow.

It is the work of the Christian parent to train his children. Their attitudes and habits, their ways of thinking and feeling and acting, should be in harmony with the belief that they are holy in Christ and belong to the Holy Spirit. "Holy in all manner of conversation" (1 Peter 1:15) is what your children are to be; their young lives should be separated from the world. They are to be consecrated to God, His Spirit, and His will.

It is as we begin to understand the word, "Your children are holy," clearly, that we will know to apply it. We will find it a word of great power in our dealings both with God and with our children. With God it will be the strength of our prayer and faith. We may be sure that when our children are called *holy,* all that is implied in the word *holy* is

268

meant for them. As we study this word in the Scriptures, we will find in God's promise "Your children are holy," the assurance that it is all for them. As we plead for the conversion of our children, we can say with holy boldness, Have You not said they are holy? We must confess how little we have realized the holiness of our children and the blessed heritage of holiness they have in us as believing parents. We must yield ourselves more than ever to train them as holy to the Lord.

A Holy Influence

This word holy will exercise its influence in our dealings with our children. We will begin to think of our home and family as His home, the dwelling place of His holiness. We will learn to look upon sin in our children, upon the spirit of the world, or conformity to it, as completely incompatible with a child whom the Holy God has set apart for holiness. We will write holiness to the Lord upon our doorposts. We will realize that the first requirement for a parent, whose children God calls holy, is that they be very holy. Personal holiness is the essential condition for raising a holy child. "Your children are holy" will lead us to look to our own position as parents. We must look to our own example and conduct as the channel through which the knowledge, love, and power of holiness are to come to them.

The words that God, Himself, spoke of Jesus may be said of each child who is born: "that holy thing which shall be born of thee" (Luke 1:35).

We shall realize that nothing but a life entirely under the leading of the Spirit of holiness can equip us for watching over and training the children God has given us.

A Parent's Prayer

O blessed God, You have revealed Yourself as the Holy One who makes holy. Your Son is the Holy One, Your Spirit is the Spirit of holiness. You call Your people Your holy ones. Of their little ones You say, "Your children are holy." Lord God, Your words are never empty like men's words; they are full of meaning, of life, and of power. Oh, make these words of Yours quick and powerful in our hearts, that we may understand and rejoice in the infinite blessing they bring us. And grant, Lord, that as we love and train our children, as we pray and believe for them, may this be our one motive and aim: that they may be holy to the Lord, realizing and showing forth the glory of His holiness. Amen.

Chapter 44

THE REIGN OF LOVE

"Ye fathers, provoke not your children to wrath"—Ephesians 6:4.

"Fathers, provoke not your children to anger, lest they be discouraged"—Colossians 3:21.

"Charity suffereth long, and is kind. . .seeketh not her own, is not easily provoked"—1 Corinthians 13:4,5.

"Teach the young women. . .to love their children" —Titus 2:4.

The apostle Paul noticed how sadly child rearing often suffers from a lack of love. In his general epistles, Paul speaks especially to fathers. On the two occasions in which he names them, he repeats the warning to them not to provoke their children to wrath. Paul's words suggest that a child is often very provoking and that a father often allows himself to be provoked. The result, then, is that he again provokes the child to wrath. Instead of being the help and the strength of his child in seeking what is good, the father discourages and hinders him. Paul's warning shows us the difficulty of giving reproof or punishment in the right spirit, and the need for patience, wisdom and self-control. The secret of a parent's rule is that it is to be a *reign of love*.

The Father's Role

Paul especially addresses his remarks to *fathers*. They are expected to take a part in the management of the children. There are many fathers who neglect this responsibility. They try to transfer the responsibility to the mother. When returning home from the day's labor, they do not feel inclined to trouble themselves. The children are regarded as a burden rather than as a responsibility given by the Lord.

God has joined the weakness and gentleness of the mother with the firmness and strength of the father. As each parent takes his share in the work, and becomes the helper of the other, the divine blessing can be expected. In addition to the daily family devotions, there should be times when father and mother join in reading, conversation, and prayer concerning the training of their children. One half-hour a week set apart for this purpose, if it were only for one year, would bring a rich reward. It would supply a training school for parents and draw attention to many important lessons. It would give the opportunity for the mother to receive the father's help and guidance. It would bring blessings on both marital and parental love, of which Peter speaks: "Ye husbands, dwell with (your wives) according to knowledge, giving honour unto the wife, as unto the weaker vessel, and as being heirs together of the grace of life; that your prayers be not hindered" (1 Peter 3:7). Let every father accept his calling to take his part in the training of the children.

The Father's Need For Patience

"Ye fathers, provoke not your children to wrath." This usually happens when the child has first provoked the father. A child is sometimes disobedient, often thoughtless, so that even what was well-meaning may be the cause for annoyance. It is only when the nature of the child is carefully and lovingly taken into account that the parent will be able patiently to bear with him and train him.

It is the privilege and honor of the parent to have this immortal spirit entrusted to his care through whom God is to make something of beauty and of glory for Himself. Parents should not be surprised by their child's willfulness which may test their tempers and patience. Parents will see the need for preparing themselves for their holy work by faith in Him who equips us for every work He gives us to do.

"Ye fathers, provoke not your children to wrath." There is much in some children that is provoking and much in some fathers that is easily provoked. Try not to give in to such provocation. This has been the ruin of many a child. It is impossible to train a child without self-control. "Ye have need of patience" (Hebrews 10:36). "Let

273

patience have her perfect work" (James 1:4).

The life of the Christian is meant by the Father in heaven, under the guidance of the Holy Spirit, to be one of watchfulness and self-examination. In home life these practices are especially necessary. The sudden outbreaks of temper in children, the little annoyances arising from their disobedience or neglect or mistakes, are all occasions on which a father needs the love that is not easily provoked. *God meant the rule of the family to be like His own, a reign of law inspired by love.*

"Ye fathers, provoke not your children to wrath." However provoking the child may be, the father must see to it that he does not provoke the child to wrath. One provocation leads to another: an angry father makes an angry child. In each human heart there is an innate sense of the dignity of government and the duty of submission to authority. The calm, quiet assertion of authority by the parent helps the child to acknowledge the justice of his punishment. However, instead of calmly disciplining the child, the parent gives way to anger and passion with a sharp reproof or hasty punishment. When this happens, the child also becomes angry and upset about an infliction which he does not understand.

The parent is the teacher and example appointed of God to meet and conquer outbursts of his anger by the gentle firmness of love. How sad when the very opposite is the case. When a father's hasty anger inflames a child's emotions, he provokes his child to wrath!

Encourage Your Child

"That they be not discouraged." In the struggle between good and evil that goes on in the child, he should be encouraged to believe that the victory of the good is within his reach, that goodness is possible and pleasant. To inspire a child with holy confidence in what he can accomplish is one of the blessed secrets of success in training. In training a horse, extreme care is taken never to overwork it, or give it a load that might lead to failure. At each difficult place you see its master ready to inspire it with confidence. The horse must not know that it cannot succeed.

Parents must not cause the child to be discouraged by thinking that his immaturity is not taken into account or that his ideas are not regarded as being important. To keep the child from feeling he has not received the help or the justice he expects requires love, which children all too little receive, and thoughtfulness, which parents too little bestow.

Discipline Yourself To Love

"Ye fathers provoke not your children to wrath." The training of a child is a holier work than many think. It needs self-discipline above everything else. This was one of the reasons God created the family, and it is one of its chief blessings. Without knowing it, your child is God's schoolmaster to bring you nearer to Christ. The child, in his tenderness and lovingness, calls forth the love of your heart, but his waywardness and willfulness call for it even more. They put it to the test and train you in patience and gentleness. Parents must endeavor to have every reproof and every punishment guided by love; so that through it all, the child may really be encouraged to be good.

It is not by reproof and punishment, however gently and wisely administered, that parents will keep their children from getting provoked or discouraged. This is but the negative side; the positive is of more importance. Prevention is better than cure. Cultivate in yourself and the child that state of mind which removes the possibility for provocation or discouragement. Endeavor to be calm, gentle, and kind and to promote these same feelings in the child.

Show interest in the things that they enjoy and enter into their state of mind and feeling. Expect the child to imitate your spirit and temperament, and instinctively to yield themselves to influence. Try to maintain the rule of love—not merely natural parental love, but love as a principle of action that is carefully cultivated in your family life. Then the children will catch this spirit of love and become your helpers in making your home the reflection of love for which the heavenly Father guides and trains His children.

A Parent's Prayer

Gracious God and Father, I come to You with the humble confession of my sin. How often sin in the child has only been met by sin in the parent and brings out new sin which discourages the child. Help me to encourage my child to believe that he can be good and conquer his sinful ways. O God, we ask You especially for a baptism of love, of Your own love. Give us holy wisdom and patience in meeting each little outbreak of the evil nature in our children. Give us the power to inspire our child with confidence in us and the victory of good. O God, help us to train our children after Your mind and to be a pleasure to You. Amen.

Chapter 45

TRAINING CHILDREN FOR THE LORD

"Ye fathers. . .bring up your children in the nurture and admonition of the Lord"—Ephesians 6:4.

We know how important it is to distinguish between instruction and education, between teaching and training. *Teaching* is the communication of knowledge, secular or religious. *Training* is the development of the abilities, both intellectual and moral, which help the child really do and be what the teaching has presented to him. The two words the apostle Paul uses correspond exactly to our expressions. We could translate this verse to say, "Nurture them in the training and teaching of the Lord."

Training Our Children

Let us first note the spirit which must be present in the upbringing of our children: "Bring them up in the nurture and the *admonition of the Lord.*" Our children are the Lord's. Their whole education must be motivated by this thought: we must train them for Him, according to His will and in His spirit. This must be our aim: Jesus Christ, the Son of God, as our Lord and Master, with His personal presence and His love, must rule in our heart and home. We must educate our children as "unto the Lord." We must educate our children to know and love Him, to obey His will, and to serve Him. This can only be done as we study His will and the rules He has laid down in His Word concerning parental duty. We must wait for His Spirit to guide and to sanctify us for our work. Our nurturing of our children is to be the nurture of the Lord.

In the life of the child, his emotional nature, with all its sensitivity, is developed first. To regulate this emotional nature, the Creator has given two great powers, that of willing and knowing. *Training* seeks to influence the will, because it is the power which really makes a person an individual. *Teaching* supplies the knowing by which the willing is to be guided and strengthened. The nurture of the Lord is to bring up the child that he may be a vessel equipped for the Master's use, with every ability of spirit, soul, and body prepared for doing His will. The training and teaching must work in harmony to obtain this blessed objective. The purpose of all instruction is the forming of the will.

Developing Self-Control In The Child

The word education is often used to refer to what is merely instruction. I have used the word discipline to give the idea the apostle intended.

The foundation of a useful and happy life will be found in the habit of order and self-control, the ready submission to law and obedience to duty. When knowing and doing right rule the child's life, then one of the chief goals of education has been attained. Discipline uses the means and exercises the power needed for securing this result. The discipline of the Lord refers to the child's whole being, spirit, soul, and body. Whatever contributes to the healthy development of our abilities is included in the nurture of the Lord.

Order is heaven's first law throughout the universe. Everything must submit to law. The power of self-control must be cultivated in the child. The parent has to prepare the home in which the Spirit of God is to dwell. The habit of order cultivated in a little child in external things will carry over into his intellectual training. It can also become a mighty force in his moral and spiritual life.

Orderliness leads to decision of character, firmness of purpose, and strength of will. In submitting to order in the external, the child learns that for everything there are things he *must* do. Let every parent seek to discipline his child to develop the habit of sensing the rightness of order and decision. These will become ruling principles in which other natural virtues will easily find their place.

Developing Habits In The Child

Then comes the legal virtues—those distinctly commanded in God's law. These are obedience, honesty, justice, and love. Parents must remind themselves how repeated single acts often become habits. They must remember that habits have the power to emphasize the principles that underlie the acts. Our moral, like our physical efforts, are strengthened by exercise. In the child's early years, conscience may be so disciplined that it becomes habitually tender and ready to act. The innate sense of right and wrong, the feeling of guilt and shame following sin, the authority of God's Word—all these are appealed to in nurturing the child for the Lord.

There are other virtues that belong more distinctly to the New Testament. These are the faith and love of Jesus, the indwelling and leading of the Holy Spirit, self-denial, holiness, and Christlike humility. All this is not to be only a matter of teaching, but the children are to be trained in these areas. To be temples of God through the Holy Spirit and be equipped for the service of the Lord Jesus must be the aim of the divine nurture in which we seek to bring up our children.

Establishing Authority By Example

For such training to be successful, it is absolutely necessary that there be authority. The nurture must be in the discipline of the Lord. It is not enough that the parent assert the right God has given him. The authority derived from God must become a personal possession by the influence the parent acquires over the child. The parent must prove himself worthy of his position. His true authority will depend upon the strength of his moral character. To acquire such influence must be a matter of study, effort, and prayer. This is true of all parents who wish to govern their children, not by force, but in the power of a life that proves they are worthy of that position.

The secret of influence and authority is a life in which we ourselves exhibit what we would ask of our children. A life of childlike trust in the Father's love, of submission to His authority and surrender to His training, will make itself felt throughout the home. It will make us more sensitive to their childlike needs and shortcomings. It will make the children aware of our teachable spirit and our quiet resting in the divine rule. The nurture of our children will be to us and to them truly the Lord's nurture. God nurtures us by means of them. He nurtures them by means of us.

A Parent's Prayer

Blessed Father, we ask for grace to combine the teaching of our children with the discipline that trains them to walk in it. We want to mold our children's character to have order and self-control. We want them to learn submission to law and authority, in which they will find the secret of happiness. We want to give their body and mind such a healthy development that they may be useful instruments for Your Holy Spirit. Blessed Father, we look to You for the grace we need to do this work. We will trust You to show each of us where we are in danger of falling short of Your perfect plan. We will trust in You to accept our childlike desire to obey You and to bless our home, in spite of our failings. We claim the presence of Jesus our Lord. We claim the power of a full salvation for us and our children. Amen.

Chapter 46

WHY CHILDREN ARE NOT SAVED

"A bishop then must be. . .one that ruleth well his own house, having his children in subjection with all gravity; (for if a man know not how to rule his own house, how shall he take care of the church of God?). . .Let the deacons be the husbands of one wife, ruling their children and their own houses well"—1 Timothy 3:2,4,5,12.

Among the qualifications for the offices of bishop, elder, or deacon in the early Church the state of their household was taken into consideration. Failure in this area was sufficient to prevent them from holding the office for which they were otherwise qualified. It reminds us once again of the closeness of the link between parents and children, and the unity of the home as a whole. From the household you can judge what the parents are: the parents make it what it is. The household is the outgrowth and the expression of the parents' lives; the mirror in which their hidden failures are revealed.

Some may be inclined to doubt the truth of this

statement. They have often heard of godly parents whose children have turned out badly. Is all the blame to be put on the parents? We have no power to change the evil nature. It is grace alone that can do it. Is it not going too far to put the blame of unbelieving or unruly children on the parents? Is it not too extreme to consider a father unfit for holding office in the Church of God, just because his own household is not what it should be? Yet, this is what the Holy Spirit does. He teaches Paul to connect unbelieving and unruly children with the failure of the parent's authority in the home. The failure at home makes the parent unfit for church office. Let us search for the causes of failure in the parents' governing of the home.

Lack Of Self-Control

The first answer may be suggested to us by the words of Paul. He associates failure at home with failure in the Church. We may go a step backward and connect failure in the family to failure in the parent. The problem in the home reveals a problem in its headship. We have more than once seen that the secret of home rule is self-rule. We must, first, be ourselves what we want our children to be.

The wonderful power of the will with which man has been endowed was meant to make him his own master. Yet, there are many Christian parents to whom real self-control in daily life is quite foreign! It is not the thought of God's will, nor the rule of their own will, that guides and decides their conduct. Instead, in their conversation and actions, in their likes and dislikes, they are led away by the feelings of the moment. Because they believe that their prayers will be heard, they hope for the salvation of their children. And yet, their influence is setting up a most effective barrier against God's grace. They allow their own moods or tempers to affect their language and conduct. Their actions contradict their profession of being the servants of God's will.

All Christian parents must learn that quiet self-control is one of the first conditions of success in our own spiritual life. As we calmly seek to be guided by God's Spirit, we will also be successful in influencing our children. "In quietness and in confidence shall be your strength" (Isaiah 30:15). The strong influence of this restfulness will be felt greatest in the family life.

Failure To Rule

There may be other reasons for this failure in the home. A Christian parent may not be lacking in self-control, and still fail. The reason may very possibly be found in his neglect of the duty of ruling. With some this may stem from an entire ignorance of the importance of the position the parent occupies. They have never thought seriously of the extent to which the souls, wills, and characters of the children are in their hands. They have never taken the trouble to consider carefully the work entrusted to them. They may pray earnestly at times that their children may be saved.

However, they do not know that it is more important to pray daily that they, themselves, be prepared to properly guide their children.

With others the neglect of the duty to rule rests on mistaken principles. They admire a strong will. In the self-assertion of a child's will, they often see nothing but cause for amusement or admiration. They wish to see their child grow up with a strong, bold character. They would not for any reason weaken his will. They do not know that a wayward will is a curse! A will that masters itself to be obedient is the truly strong will. It is no wonder that strong-willed children later on become disobedient or unruly.

With others the neglect of the duty to rule comes from simple weakness and laziness. They admit that it is their duty, but it is difficult and takes too much time and thought. They find it too much of a burden to punish or restrain the child. Thinking they are being tenderhearted, the authority with which they have been entrusted of God is neglected and abused. Let parents take time and thought to realize that to rule a child is distinctly God's command. The time and labor spent in cultivating this grace will be richly rewarded.

Lack of Faith

There are other parents who do rule themselves and do seek to rule their children and still have failed. The cause for their failure is deeper: they lack true faith and consecration. There are some children who can be easily ruled. There are others with nervous temperaments or rebellious attitudes to defy control.

Child raising is a work in which the parents are meant to be God's servants, His fellow-workers. To really work with God means to walk closely with Him. The parent who is completely given up to Him, and seeks undividedly to do His will, will be given faith to live in the assurance that God, Himself, will do the work. The spirit of the world is the most secret but most certain hindrance to true faith. Let the surrender of ourselves and our children be complete and unreserved. We will find God to be our covenant-helper in training our children. With Him on our side, we will prevail. To have power with Him in prayer is the sure guarantee of victory with the child.

Parents, the work entrusted to us is holier than we know. The precious child, so delicate, so wonderfully made, so marred by sin already, and so exposed to its power, is of inconceivable worth. To take charge of an immortal soul, to train a will for God and eternity, makes us want to decline such a great responsibility. But we cannot. If we are parents, the duty is given to us. But, thank God, sufficient grace is prepared and promised to us. If we do give our home and life to God to come in and rule, He will take possession. Then, by the gentle influence of His Holy Spirit, they will bow their wills to Him.

The training that we receive from ruling our children will be the best preparation for our ruling in the Church. We must deny ourselves in order to acquire real influence and power to rule our children. If we do this, He will consider us worthy of influence and power with our fellowmen and in His Church. Faithfulness in the home rule will bring opportunities to take care of the Church of God.

A Parent's Prayer

O Lord, You have ordained that in each home on earth, Your heavenly rule should have its reflection. You have given to parents power and authority over their children to rule in Your name. You have promised to give us wisdom and strength for maintaining that authority and ruling our children well. We have to confess with shame how often this holy trust of ruling in Your name has been neglected and abused. We ask You to forgive us. We ask You to deliver us from all that hinders that rule. May a holy self-rule equip us for a happy home rule. We desire to make the work You have given us a pleasure and to prepare ourselves carefully for doing it well. Be our teacher and our help. Lord Jesus, we yield our homes and our children to be completely Yours. You are able to keep that which we commit to You. Keep our homes as Your sacred dwelling-place, where we and our children serve You in righteousness and love, in peace and in great joy. Amen.

Chapter 47

CHILDREN AND SCRIPTURE

"I call to remembrance the unfeigned faith that is in thee, which dwelt first in thy grandmother Lois, and thy mother Eunice"—2 Timothy 1:5.

"Continue thou in the things which thou hast learned and hast been assured of, knowing. . . that from a child thou hast known the holy scriptures, which are able to make thee wise unto salvation through faith which is in Christ Jesus"—2 Timothy 3:14,15.

If we connect these two passages, we find in them the true relationship between children and Scripture. Between the sincere faith of the mother and grandmother, and the faith of Timothy, the connecting link was Scripture. Scripture needs the believing parent as its messenger. The believing parent needs Scripture as the vehicle for the communication of his faith. A parent teaching the word of faith may expect the child's faith to be the fruit of his labors.

God has planned for the Word to be brought to

sinners through the Holy Spirit dwelling in His saints. The same Spirit dwells in the Word and in the child of God. In the combined action of the two, the Word is made a blessing to others. One of the highest honors God gives to the believing parent is his role as the minister of His holy Word to his children. The sincere faith of a father or mother is a faith which lives according to the Word and speaks of it in the power of personal testimony and experience. This kind of faith will be used of God to awaken the child's faith. In genuine, living faith, there is something contagious. The life of the Spirit breathes in it and makes its words a blessing. This truth suggests precious lessons a parent should seek to learn.

Teach Children To Believe God's Word

In the Old Testament, God sought above everything else to train His saints to be men of faith. There is nothing more pleasing to Him than faith. Faith is the soul's surrender to God, to hear what He says, to take what He gives, to receive what He works, to be entirely at His disposal. Faith in God begins with faith in His Word. The most important habit a parent can cultivate in a child is that of a trustful acceptance of all that God has said.

In an age of doubt and questioning, teach the child to accept what he cannot understand. Teach him to believe, even what appears to be mysterious and contrary to reason, because God who is wise and great has said it. Teach him to believe in His love, in the gift of His Son, and in the life through Him. Teach the child to accept these as realities which come true to us as our faith simply trusts the Word and is assured of what it says. Teach him day by day to look upon every promise, every truth in the Word, as the food of faith, meant to make our faith and our life stronger. Parents, a child is naturally trusting. You must guide this young trust to that Word which never fails. The child wants to trust and the Word wants to be trusted—let your faith bring them into contact.

Teach Children To Know God's Word

Faith depends upon knowledge. Timothy had known the sacred writings as able to make him wise unto salvation. If the grace of God is to save us, it must teach us. It is wisdom from above. We must love God with the mind as well as the heart. Let the parent seek to give the child a clear and intelligent understanding of the great truths of salvation God has revealed. He must not entrust this work to the school or church.

Let family worship be conducted in a way that will help the children to know and understand God's Word. When you are reading from the Bible, always try to make it clear at what stage in history the event took place. Take time to lodge in the child's mind the truths and the history of the Bible. Help them to store in their memories some of God's own words. Do not be content with the child's learning and saying his memorized portions at certain times, because it is often forgotten as soon as said. But seek to have some of these portions, by frequent repetition, so rooted in the mind that nothing can erase them. Teach the child to know the Bible and to be at home in it. To be taught by the parent's faith to know the sacred writings is an inestimable blessing.

Teach Children To Love God's Word

This is more difficult than to teach the child to believe and to know it. There is often the assent of faith and an interest in the knowledge of Scripture, with very little real love for it. To teach this is no easy task. The first requirement is, of course, that we love it ourselves. "Oh, how I love Thy law" (Psalm 119:97) is an expression which many earnest believers are afraid to utter. Love and joy ever go together: what I love, I rejoice to possess. Reverence and respect for God's Word, the earnest study of it, and the desire to be guided by it— these are good. However, they do not necessarily breathe that bright spirit of delight which says to God, "Oh, how I love Thy law!"

Yet a child's heart is especially susceptible to love. Childhood is the age of feeling and impression. A parent's holy, tender love for the Word of God will be the surest means of inspiring the child's love. Let this be a distinct matter of desire and prayer. Seek to guide the child in such a way that he may not only like the Bible for its stories and its study, but truly and heartily love it as the Father's word. This will, indeed, be the result of divine grace, and the preparation for other spiritual blessings.

Teach Children To Obey God's Word

God connects all believing, knowing, and loving, with doing. Obedience is God's test of righteousness and reality. Teach the child the Father's standard of conduct. In our ordinary Christianity, children are taught to believe that God's commandments are unpleasant. The Bible must not be like a rule book continually holding us in check, keeping us from what we would like and demanding what is difficult. No! With our children we must take an entirely different position.

As the Father's redeemed ones, we must say, with His Son, "I delight to do Thy will, O my God; yea, Thy law is within my heart" (Psalm 40:8). It is His covenant promise to work this in us and our children. Then they will learn from us how impossible it is to read the Father's Word and not do it. Our study of it with them will have this as its one purpose: we want to know and do the will of God.

The practice of family worship is found in almost every Christian family. Every day a portion of God's holy Word is read together. But in that reading there is often little power or blessing. Many Christian parents look more to his private reading for spiritual nourishment. Yet, the daily gathering of the family around the Word of God could also be a blessed time of refreshment and nourishment!

We take great care to have a properly prepared meal placed on the breakfast table, so that each child is served just what he needs. We need to take the same care to see that the children really receive and enjoy the feeding with the divine Word. Let parents strive to have their family worship time planned in such a way as to lead the children into the Lord's presence. There they will be fed with the bread each one requires and receive the Father's blessing for the day. Parents should take time to prepare for reading the Word with their family. God's Word should be read reverently, as abiding in His presence and waiting on His Spirit. Beware of the hurry which gives just enough time for the hasty reading of a chapter. This can make family worship a dead formality and create a careless attitude toward the Word and God Himself. Parents should spend a few moments calling attention to what God says in His Word. After making personal application, the children should be encouraged to take and keep the Word, practicing it in their daily life.

Parents, God's Word is your child's heritage from the Father in heaven. And you are commissioned to lead him into the knowledge and the love and possession of its treasures. Make it a matter of earnest prayer that you may wisely and rightly do this. Let that word dwell richly in you in all wisdom. In giving His promises, Jesus said, "If ye abide in Me, and My words abide in you" (John 15:7). Let your life be one of unfeigned faith, that lives and delights in doing God's Word. Then this faith will pass on into your children. The quiet confidence that comes from God's Word is a power that makes itself felt with our children. If you feel that you do not know how to bring the Word to them, do not be discouraged, you have God to do the work, to make the Word effective. Pray and believe for the Holy Spirit's working. He will make the Word, which you speak and live in unfeigned faith, the seed of faith to Your children, too.

A Parent's Prayer

Gracious God, we ask for the grace of wisdom, faith, and patient faithfulness, to bring Your Word day by day to our children. May our family worship every day be a holy time of communion with You. May we use this time to lead our children into Your presence, to hear Your voice speak and to receive Your teaching. Lord, we yield ourselves to the supremacy and the power of Your Holy Word. Let it so abide in us, that our life may be the shining forth of its holy light. Let us be so full of faith, love, and obedience to God's Word, that our dear children learn from their youth to love and believe and obey it, too. Father, forgive us for failing to do this in the past. By Your mighty power make it so now. Amen.

Chapter 48

BELIEVING CHILDREN

"If any (elders) be blameless, the husband of one wife, having faithful children not. . .unruly"—Titus 1:6.

God expects that the children of believers should be believers, too. There is nothing so honoring or pleasing to God as our belief in Him. Nothing so opens the way for His blessing and love to flow in and take possession of us as our belief in Him. The very object and purpose of God in the institution of the parental covenant is that believing parents should train believing children. They are the children of the promise. God and His grace are theirs in promise, but a promise has value only if it is believed. Parents who truly believe will understand that it is their privilege and their duty to train "faithful children" who believe.

Children—Heirs Of The Promise

We have seen how, on the day of Pentecost with the outpouring of the Holy Spirit, Peter announced that the foundation principle of God's covenant with Abraham was to remain unchanged. Children were still to be regarded as the heirs of the promise. Family life, as ordained by God was still to be the channel for the transmission of the blessing of the Spirit. Faith was not to be an individual thing, but to embrace the household.

It is in harmony with this that we so often find in the book of Acts mention made of the household. "Cornelius. . .feared God with all his house" (Acts 10:1,2). "Lydia. . .was baptized, and her household" (Acts 16:14,15). To the jailer of Philippi Paul said, "Believe. . .and thou shalt be saved, and thy house. . .and he was baptized, and all his, straightway. . .and he rejoiced, believing in God with all his house" (Acts 16:31,33,34). "Crispus, the chief ruler of the synagogue, believed on the Lord with all his house" (Acts 18:8). In the Epistles of Paul we find that he uses the expression, "the church in thy house" four times. He does not say the church assembling in thy house, but "the church which is in thy house," referring evidently to the circle of believers constituting the family. Although in these cases no express mention is made of children, the idea of a household assures us that the children were present, too.

It is clear to Paul that believing parents ought to have believing children. When such is not the case, he regards it as an indication that there has been some failure on the part of the parents. He concludes that their own faith and life has not been what it should be, and they are at once debar-

ones of faith. Let us review the lessons God wants to teach us.

Children Can Be Believers

Trusting—the power of simply believing what is told and of resting on what love has promised—is one of the most beautiful traits of true childlikeness. It is this wonderful power of a child's heart that must be guided heavenward and led to cling to God and His Word, to Jesus and His love. There is nothing more natural to children than to believe. It is through a parent's faith that the Holy Spirit loves to take possession of the child's faith. As the child grows, his faith grows, becoming a deep and hidden root of life that clings to the blessed Savior.

God expects our children to grow up believers. We ought to expect this, too. It is the very nature of faith in God to seek to think as He thinks. Faith counts upon Him to do what is impossible with man and nature. We must be convinced that God will use us as the channels of His Holy Spirit to fulfill the promise to our children. This confidence that our children will grow up true believers will exercise its influence on us and on them. It will daily call us to a life of pure holiness and consecration. This will create an atmosphere of faith which our children will breathe and live. In our homes God expects there to be children who believe.

consecration. This will create an atmosphere of faith which our children will breathe and live. In our homes God expects there to be children who believe.

A Child's Faith

The proof that our children are believers will be their conduct. Paul writes, "elders having faithful children, not unruly." Faith is always perfected by works. Like every other function of life, it can grow and become strong only by action. A life of faith is always a life of obedience. A child's faith must prove itself in a child's obedience; that is, his obedience to the parents. Children who are allowed to be unruly, disobedient, and self-willed will quickly lose their childlike faith.

Faith is surrender. I yield myself entirely to the influence of the words I hear, of the promise I receive, of the person I trust. Faith in Jesus is entire surrender to Him, to be ruled, influenced, and mastered by Him. Faith in Jesus is surrender to Him and His will. Faith in Jesus to be saved is surrender to let Him save us in the way He has opened up, the way of trusting, loving, holy obedience. Let parents seek to lead the little one's simple faith in Jesus to this surrender. Let them claim the child's obedience to themselves as obedience to Jesus. Let them educate the child to obey conscience in Jesus' name. Then their home will be the happy proof that believing children are not unruly.

Causes Of Unbelief

If our children do not believe, let us look at ourselves for the cause. There must be something wrong with our consecration. It may be that the spirit of the world has so invaded the heart and home, that the parent's life trains the children to have faith in the world, to surrender to its spirit and rule. Or it may be that, while we are earnestly engaged in religion and religious work, there is little true spirituality. There is no joy, love, or power of holiness which alone makes religion a reality. It may be that religion has become an occupation like any other, and the holy presence of Jesus has not been felt by our children. Or there may have been failure in our not devoting ourselves to the holy task of training our children. We may have entrusted the work to others and neglected the self-denial and the study needed to equip ourselves for the work of ruling and guiding our children in the ways of the Lord. Let us seek very honestly and very earnestly to discover the reason for our failure. We are believers, we have a faithful God; yet, we have not what He claims, "faithful children, not unruly."

God calls us to heart searching and confession. Even if we have children who believe, but their faith is not as devoted as we would wish, let us look to God with a new surrender. Our home life needs the power of a true consecration. Our homes need the warm light of the Savior's love and the joy of His near presence shining from us. This

301

is the secret of successful child raising.

Each new step in the path of entire separation to God is felt in the family. If there are circumstances and influences that make this seem impossible, let us remember what faith can do. Faith can bring Almighty God and His power onto the scene. It is the faith of entire surrender that our homes need, and that will transform them into what God would have them to be.

Let us remember that there is no power so mighty as that of a quiet, restful faith. Faith knows that God has given what we have asked, that He has taken charge of what we have entrusted to Him, and that in His own hidden, silent ways He is already working out what He has undertaken. Parents who are believers, who believe with their whole heart and strength and life, will have "faithful children, not unruly."

A Parent's Prayer

Blessed Lord God, we thank You for each message that reminds us of what You would have our children to be. We ask You to print deep in our hearts the truth that in every believing home You expect and seek believing children. Lord, as trees of Your planting, we yield to You the fruit You seek. When You do not find this fruit, convict us of the sin that is the cause of this failure. Whether it is unbelief or worldliness, the lack of ruling well or the lack of living well, reveal the sin, that it may be confessed and cast out. Reveal, especially, how it is the lack of our undivided consecration to

Your will that is the secret cause of all our failure. Lord, it is Your presence with us that will strengthen our faith and give us children who believe. We open our homes to You. Come in and reign. Be our joy and gladness every day. We have yielded ourselves to live each moment under Your rule. Give us children who believe, children who in the power of faith You can use for Your glory. Amen.

Chapter 49

I AND THE CHILDREN

"Behold I and the children which God hath given me"—Hebrews 2:13.

These words were originally used by the prophet Isaiah: "Behold, I and the children whom the Lord hath given me are for signs and for wonders in Israel" (Isaiah 8:18). The prophet and his family were to be God's witnesses to certain great truths which God wanted His people not to forget. In the Epistle to the Hebrews, these words of the Holy Spirit are put into the mouth of Christ as His confession of His relationship to those whom He is not ashamed to call His brethren. They are words which the Holy Spirit still uses as the language of the believing parent who presents himself with his children before the Lord. As we draw our meditations to a close, these words invite us to review all that the Word has taught us of the purpose and the promise of our God concerning the raising and training of our children. We have learned that our hope looks to the fulfillment of all God has led us to expect.

The Foundation For Our Faith

"Behold, I and the children which God hath given me!" Let this be the language of a deep and living faith, as we think of the wonderful foundation of our unity. I am one with my children in virtue of God's eternal purpose, established when He created man and instituted the family. He meant for the parent to produce children in his own likeness, to impart his own life and spirit to them, to have one life with them. When sin entered, the promise and the covenant were given to restore the blessing that had been lost. The parent was in faith to receive for the child, and communicate to him the grace God has bestowed. In virtue of that promise, I am one with my children, and my children are one with me, in the enjoyment of the love and the life that comes in Jesus.

In that faith I present myself before the Father and I say, "Father! Behold, I and the children whom Thou hast given me." *Thou* hast given them to me, with a divine giving, to be inseparably and eternally one with me. God has given them to me, in the power of the complete redemption of His Son, with the sure and full promise of His Holy Spirit. God has given them to me to keep and train for Him, and then present them before Him as mine and His, too. In this faith I want day by day to look upon my little flock and believe that they are one with me in the possession of all the promises and blessings of the covenant.

When it may seem as if they are not growing up

as one with me in Christ, my faith will still say, "Behold, I and the children Thou hast given me." When the thought of my past sin and neglect in my training of them makes me feel guilty, I will look to the blood sprinkled on the doorposts of my home. I will look to the precious all-availing blood, that cleanses all my sin and say, "Behold, I and the children whom Thou hast given me." We are one, we must be one through Your grace, we will be one to all eternity.

Faith Works By Love

In Jesus Christ nothing is accomplished except by faith working in love. "Behold, I and the children God hath given me." When spoken in loving faith, these words become the inspiration of love for the work God has committed to it. The bond between a parent and child is a double one—there is the unity of life and of love. This natural parental love cares for, trains, and nurtures the child. It is this love that God takes and sanctifies for His service. It is this love that becomes the strength for the difficult and yet delightful work the parent has to do.

Love is always self-surrender and self-sacrifice. It gives itself away to the beloved one and desires to enter into his life; it becomes one with him. True love has no rest apart from perfect union with the beloved—all it has must be shared together. God calls Christian parents to love their children, to identify themselves with them, to seek and claim their salvation as much as their own. As the Spirit of Christ takes possession of the heart, the parent accepts the call. The parent is ready to sacrifice everything to make his children partakers of this great salvation. The parent learns to say with new meaning, "Behold, I and the children which God hath given me."

I and the children! I am: the author of their life; the framer of their character; the keeper of their souls; the trustee of their eternal destiny. I am blessed, that I may bless them. Having experienced how patient, gentle, and tender He is with my ignorance and willfulness, I can now bear with my children's weaknesses in the meekness, gentleness, and patience of Christ.

Yes, I and the children! I become more aware that, in the unity of love, what I am, the children may and will be. The more tenderly my love for them is stirred up, the more I feel that I need to be all and only the Lord's. This will fill me with an unselfish love, which will give me the strength to live for the children that God has given me.

Looking Forward To Heaven

When faith and love have spoken, hope will have courage to say, "Behold, I and the children which the Lord hath given me!" We are inseparably and eternally one. Hope is the child of faith and love. Faith is hope's strength for waiting and watching, love is its strength for willing and working. Hope ever looks forward. It sees even in this life, when things are dark, the Unseen God coming through the clouds to fulfill His Word.

Hope sings the song of victory, when others see nothing but defeat. Amid all the struggles through which you may see a beloved child passing, amid all trials of faith and patience, hope speaks: In His word do I hope: I will hope continually, and will praise You yet more and more. Hope inspires the children when they are discouraged in their fight with evil.

Hope looks forward to each child in the family being not only a saved one, but a sanctified one, equipped for the Master's service here on earth. Hope rejoices in the assurance of knowing they will have an unbroken family circle in heaven. Hope even now causes the parents to tremble with joy as they think of the privilege that awaits them in heaven. They think of coming forward to fall down and worship and say, "Father, behold! here am I, and the children which You have given me." May God teach us to rejoice in this hope! "Now the God of hope fill you with all joy and peace in believing, that ye may abound in hope, through the power of the Holy Ghost" (Romans 15:13).

"Behold I and the children which God hath given me." Beloved fellow-believers, whom God has honored to be parents, let us seek to have the spirit of these words breathed throughout our family life. It is God who has given us the children. It is He who regards them as one with us in His covenant and blessing. It is His love that calls and equips us for a life of self-sacrifice and unselfishness. It is His grace which will give success to our efforts to be one with our children in the power of faith and love and hope. In God's sight and promise we are one. In our life and love and labor let us be one with them, too, for we will be one through the glory of eternity.

A Parent's Prayer

Our gracious Father, we thank You for all the blessed teaching of Your Holy Word concerning our children. We thank You that You have come as our teacher to equip us for teaching them. We ask You to help us to become the parents You would have us to be. O Lord, establish in our thoughts, hearts, and lives all the wonderful truths that concern the home life. We consider Your covenant and its promises as exceedingly precious to us. We treasure all the promises of Your Spirit and Your blessing as our children's sacred heritage. We accept all Your warnings and all Your instructions concerning children as the rules of our home. O Lord, open our eyes, that we may always have before us the picture of a believing home as You would have it to be. Give us the power to fulfill the Father's will and to win our children's love. Accept our consecration to be completely Yours. Come and let our home be a place where You love to dwell. Then will our home be blessed, indeed, and each of us will say with gladness, "Behold I and the child God hath given me." Even so, come, Lord Jesus. Amen.

Chapter 50

PRINCIPLES OF TRAINING FOR PARENTS

It may be helpful to parents, to young mothers especially, to give a short summary of the principles on which all training is founded. Training children is a work that cannot be performed without careful thought and determination. The infinite significance of this holy work of molding, of really forming and giving shape to an immortal spirit requires much wisdom. To accomplish this great task, we must claim the promise: "If any of you lack wisdom, let him ask of God, that giveth to all men liberally. . .and it shall be given him" (James 1:5).

1. *Training is more than teaching.* Teaching makes a child know and understand what he is to do. Training influences him and sees that he does it. Teaching deals with the child's mind. Training deals with his will.

2. *Prevention is better than cure.* True training is watching the child to help him prevent mistakes. It is *not* watching him with the intention of correcting his mistakes. The highest aim of true

training is to help the child know that he *can* obey and do right, that he can do it easily and successfully and delight in doing it.

3. *Habits must precede principles.* During the first years of a child's life, his body is constantly growing and changing. It is during this time that his lifelong habits can be formed. Habits influence the person by making the performance of certain acts easy and natural. After these are established, the way is prepared for the child to obey rules and principles.

4. *Developing a positive attitude is essential to learning.* During the early years of childhood, the child is very susceptible to his feelings and impressions. Because of this the parent must try to make doing what is right seem attractive and desirable. The child must develop a favorable attitude toward being and doing good. Without this positive attitude, habits will have little value. With it, they will be the connecting link by which habits become the actual desired will of the child.

5. *Example is better than precept.* The power of training lies not in what we say and teach, but in what we *are* and *do*. It is not the way we think, but the way we live, that makes a difference. It is not our wishes or our ideas, but our will and practice that train our children. By living a principle or ideal, we prove that we love that principle and that it is part of us. In this way, we influence the young mind to love it and to attain it, too.

6. *Love that draws is more than law that demands.* Training children requires a life of self-

311

sacrifice. It requires love that "seeketh not its own," but lives and gives of itself. God has given the wonderful gift of mother-love. When this love is directed into the right channel, it becomes the handmaid of God's redeeming love. Rules and regulations presented without love always bring about sin and bitterness. Love gives itself, with all its thought and strength, to live for others. Love breathes its own stronger and better life into the weaker one. Love inspires, and this inspiration is the secret of training.

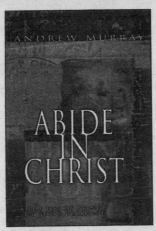

Abide in Christ
Andrew Murray

So many Christians, instead of accepting God's invitation to enter His throne room, stand alone outside the door, uncertain and ashamed. They come to Jesus as Redeemer but never go beyond the doorway to abide in Him. Andrew Murray knew what it meant to dwell in the Father's presence. Here he shares how to live daily in closer communion and fellowship with Him. Accept God's invitation to live in His blessing instead of shuffling your feet at the gate, and experience the unspeakable joy of dwelling with the King of Kings.

ISBN: 978-0-88368-860-1 • Trade • 256 pages

www.whitakerhouse.com

Healing Secrets
Andrew Murray

You can experience complete healing! Many
questions arise about divine healing, such as "Why
are some people healed while others are not?"
and "What part do doctors play in divine healing?"
Find the answers to these questions and more in
Healing Secrets. Writing from his own experience,
Andrew Murray examines what the Bible says about
sickness and how to obtain health—body, mind, and
spirit. Gain a biblical perspective on healing with the
timeless truths found in this classic.

ISBN: 978-0-88368-540-2 • Trade • 160 pages

www.whitakerhouse.com

Humility

Andrew Murray

Is your walk with God stale? Are the same old things just not working as you seek intimacy and God's power for your life? In this classic text by faith-great Andrew Murray, you will find refreshment for your spiritual journey and learn that humble dependence on God is the basis of all genuine blessing. Discover how to model your life after Jesus' life, find joy in service, and add power to your witnessing. Bring your focus back to God, and walk in His will as never before!

ISBN: 978-0-88368-178-7 • Trade • 128 pages

WHITAKER
HOUSE

www.whitakerhouse.com

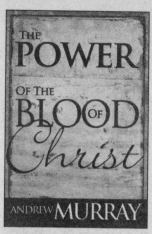

The Power of the Blood of Christ
Andrew Murray

Sure, you know that "there's power in the blood," just like the old hymn says—but are you actually experiencing that power in your daily life? Instead, are you feeling spiritually tired? Worn-out? Weak? Lifeless? Walking in your own strength instead of relying on the finished work of Christ can leave you spiritually exhausted and emotionally weary. Join Andrew Murray in this classic exploration of the blessings to be found in Christ's blood. Experience amazing breakthroughs as you daily abide in the victory secured by *The Power of the Blood of Christ!*

ISBN: 978-0-88368-242-5 • Trade • 176 pages

www.whitakerhouse.com

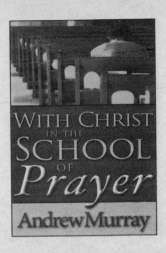

With Christ in the School of Prayer
Andrew Murray

Few books have had as much impact in calling
the church to prayer as Andrew Murray's
classic, *With Christ in the School of Prayer.* As you
saturate yourself in the timeless wisdom found
here, you will discover how to prepare yourself
for effective participation in the great privilege
Christ has extended to believers—to join
with Him in intercessory prayer.

ISBN: 978-0-88368-106-0 • Pocket • 240 pages

www.whitakerhouse.com

The Practice of God's Presence
Andrew Murray

Do you long to become the person God wants you to be? Do you wish you had more spiritual power? You can experience victory over sin, forgiveness and freedom from guilt, and a deeper understanding of your salvation. Here are six of Andrew Murray's books, filled with biblical insights that will transform your life. It is possible to trade your weakness for God's strength and power—by His grace!

ISBN: 978-0-88368-590-7 • Trade • 576 pages

www.whitakerhouse.com

Andrew Murray on Prayer
Andrew Murray

Combining seven of Andrew Murray's most treasured works on prayer, this book will give you biblical guidelines for effective communication with God. Discover essential keys to developing a vital prayer life, including how to receive clear direction from the Lord, see your unsaved loved ones come to Christ, and overcome temptation. Lovingly explained, the principles presented here will permanently transform your prayer life!

ISBN: 978-0-88368-528-0 • Trade • 656 pages

WHITAKER
HOUSE

www.whitakerhouse.com

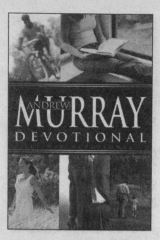

Andrew Murray Devotional
Andrew Murray

Andrew Murray's uplifting messages for each day of the year will comfort and refresh you in your walk with God. Spending time with God daily will bring a new joy and peace into your life. As you daily explore these truths excerpted from some of Murray's most treasured writings, you will connect with God's glorious power and see impossibilities turn into realities. Don't miss out on the most important part of the day—those miraculous, life-changing moments spent with your Creator.

ISBN: 978-0-88368-778-9 • Trade • 400 pages

www.whitakerhouse.com